RIVERSIDE COMMUNITY COLLEGE
1916

D0408354

THE AMERICAN WAY OF DIVORCE:
Prescriptions for Change

THE AMERICAN WAY OF DIVORCE:

Prescriptions for Change

Sheila Kessler

Nelson-Hall, Chicago

Riverside Community College
Library
4800 Magnolia Avenue
Riverside, CA 92506

Library of Congress Cataloging in Publication Data

Kessler, Sheila.
    The American way of divorce.

    Bibliography: p.
    Includes index.
    1. Divorce—United States I. Title.
HQ834.K47   301.42'84'0973   74-28078
ISBN 0-88229-234-X

Copyright © 1975 by Sheila Kessler

All rights reserved. No part of this book may be reproduced without permission in writing from the publisher, except by a reviewer who wishes to quote brief passages in connection with a review written for broadcast or for inclusion in a magazine or newspaper. For information address Nelson-Hall, Inc., Publishers, 325 West Jackson Blvd., Chicago, Ill. 60606.

Manufactured in the United States of America.

Contents

THE AMERICAN WAY
OF DIVORCE:
Prescriptions for Change

Chapter 1

Introduction

Too late. Too late for sex manuals. Too late for advice. Too late for marital counselors. Just in time for divorce.

Every year millions of couples fall into this category. According to a U.S. Public Health report approximately 1.5 million couples will physically separate each year. Some 839,000 will divorce. For every five couples who are earnestly vowing "until death do us part" another two couples are busily dissolving their bonds.

If you have gone through emotional divorce yourself; if you have been a child of divorced parents; if you are helping others work through a divorce; or if you are interested in an improved system of marriage and divorce, you will find this book helpful. Part I provides therapy. Part II enlightens. Part III focuses on badly needed reform.

Getting divorced emotionally is akin to the way a sleepwalker feels when awakening at the edge of the roof, knowing little about the journey, what caused the perambulation, or how to get down safely.

This book uncovers emotions and facts associated

with divorce. It also suggests reform. Part I delves into emotions and deals with divorce on a personal, emotional level. Part II presents facts about divorce in the United States and other societies and deals with the subject on a societal, attitudinal level. Drawing from inner thoughts and feelings revealed by scores of clients in therapy, this book presents a candid picture of the often scarring divorce process.

Society and individuals need better ways of breaking with the past. Instead of clinging to laws and relationships which once worked, we need to learn how to move on. The benefits: (1) a more adaptive individual for a highly transient and fast-paced society, and (2) a more smoothly functioning society where disrupted individuals don't waste so much valuable time in pulling themselves together.

{ Although common, divorce can be traumatic. Physical separation means leaving a formerly pleasing partner. It means leaving old friends. Often it means leaving a neighborhood and a familiar lifestyle. Habits are forcibly broken. Budgets are put under enormous strain. Families are confused and dismayed. The emotional pricetag of divorce is staggering. You may know this from personal experience. }

Subtly our society tarnishes divorced men and women. Our adversary system of law still punishes rather than rehabilitates. Lawyers, for instance, often encourage each party to take what they can get out of the hide of the other. Divorce papers are entitled *"John Smith* vs. *Mary Smith"* instead of "In the best interests of the Smith family." No extended family absorbs the recently divorced person. Competition between partners rather than cooperation is encouraged.

Married couples often feel threatened around an unattached person and make the divorced person uncomfortable. Ideals designed exclusively for the divorced person to live up to and in order to become a better single adult or single parent are practically non-existent. Judgmental attitudes of friends, their deeply-rooted emotional responses, often discriminate against the divorced person. Credit bureaus, employment opportunities and country clubs frequently exclude the divorced.

Where can a newly divorced person turn for help? States provide few provisions for divorce-counseling in their legal aspects. Scant attention has been paid to the subject of aiding someone through an emotional divorce. Few courses are taught at college which deal with divorce nonjudgmentally. Only groups such as Parents Without Partners open the door a crack and provide a place where persons can attempt to untie emotional knots. We still have a long way to go in order to assimilate these people into society.

Trauma is not, in all societies, a component of divorce. The United States has, by not dealing intelligently with it, helped to magnify the consequences and aggravate the impact. Our Puritan heritage sneaks into the picture here. Feelings of failure run rampant among newly divorced persons: "Why couldn't I make the marriage work?" "What was wrong with me that my partner rejected me?" The other side of this self-accusation is to blame the ex-spouse: "My husband ran off with another woman and left me with the three kids after twenty years of unquestioned loyalty!" "My wife drank too much and drove me insane." The emotionality of this kind of destructive thinking is not by accident. Our religious forebears very carefully developed and encouraged a system of mores that would engender guilt. Guilt helped preserve the family unit in previous centuries. But it doesn't any longer.

Our current feelings are directly linked to our own past. How? Consider a common way we have of viewing a couple recently divorced—the errant and the innocent. Reexamine you own discussions with others about a divorcing couple and see whether or not an attempt was made to determine who was at fault. Flirtation with others helps to assign guilt. For centuries, a formalized court would decide the issue. The judge would saddle the moral culprit with heavy alimony payments or total lack of monetary aid. The innocent would bear the emotional cross of being victimized. No-fault divorce obscures this sharp dichotomy. Yet our attitudes still reflect the mores from earlier history. Attitudes and values must adapt to the changing needs of modern society and its inhabitants. In addition to being destructive and immobilizing, guilt may be totally inappropriate.

Married to our past, we are oblivious to our present and blinded to our future. Social scientists have virtually omitted the emotional process of divorce from their research. Consequently we know little about it. Only one large-scale study, entitled *Women in Divorce* by William Goode, has sought to explore and validate what persons go through when divorcing. Little is known about what might prevent divorce.

Individuals need special tools for untying emotional knots. Disaffiliation as well as affiliation are learned skills. Transient friendships abound in a rootless and mobile society. Close friends and neighbors move away. Roommates part. Lovers disentangle. The entire emotional process of uncoupling takes an enormous amount of energy. Some individuals bluster through and others retain permanent emotional scars. A few make use of the experience to enhance their personalities and become more exciting, productive, creative individuals. The difference is training. If emotional disengagement has not been a part of the early learning process, the skill can still be developed.

Dissolution training is given in Part I of this book. Creative divorce does not remove the pain but rather uses it for constructive change. Stages of emotional divorce are provided to help the person organize his or her experience. The evolution of emotional divorce is given in Chapter II as the fairly common stages of (1) disappointment and disillusionment; (2) erosion; (3) detachment; (4) separation; (5) mourning; (6) second adolescence; and (7) hard work. Each of the first four stages is clarified when the constructive elements of such emotions as anger, depression, grief, guilt and helplessness become destructive. Upswing emotions appear in the return to, or second, adolescence and pour forth in feelings of an earlier carefree time. Mischievous smiles pass across the divorced person's face while relating experiments with new and exciting behaviors. A sexual smorgasbord is offered to the single who desires it. Often a person rediscovers appetites and feelings long since forgotten. Jealousy. Explorations. Courage. Vulnerability. Sensuality. Overdependency. The intricate footwork involved in dating games tickles the adolescent's fancies.

In the final stage, the reintegrated person is hard at work reaching out for new goals. Often such a person has reorganized his or her life for the better. New friends, new lifestyles, new beliefs, and more adaptive behaviors emerge in this period. Renewed self-worth and a sense of self-sufficiency propel a person into areas hitherto unexplored. Coping mechanisms have been strengthened, so the person is not so afraid of future crises. The reintegration engenders confidence, new vitality and courage. Wiser, more aware of self and others, more effective in his or her dealings with others, the person in this last stage has capitalized on the pain of divorce and transformed it into strength.

For those who get stuck between the stage of

mourning and rediscovery, the next few chapters provide emotional first-aid. The bogged-down person usually becomes involved in self-defeating behaviors, emotions and/or thoughts.

If you find yourself excessively nervous, Chapter 3, "Emotional Freedom," suggests various methods of reducing anxiety. Therapy is one. Psychiatric or psychological therapy allows the individual to drain off emotions while clarifying the real problems. Faster methods of reducing anxiety include techniques like systematic desensitization and yoga. While no simple recipes are provided, what is offered are alternative behaviors.

Chapter 4, "Purging Demons from the Mind," lists specific irrational thoughts unintentionally used by people to make themselves miserable—self-torturing thoughts such as, "It is a dire necessity to be loved," and "I can't stand to live alone." The swirling anxieties and uncertainties of postdivorce fuel these emotion-laden thoughts.

Breaking inappropriate habits may cause problems for some. "Behavior Control," Chapter 5, begins with suggestions for easier habit-breaking. The neophyte breaking dysfunctional habits is often overwhelmed with the powerful inertia of old habits. Habits such as calling your ex before making a decision about Johnny when you are supposed to be working hard at independence; such as visiting the tennis club on the same nights your ex does when it is extremely painful to meet; such as dwelling on the topic of your ex with your uninterested date. There's nothing big about these behaviors. But when added together, they can spell disaster.

Behavioral coping breaks down into manageable units the identity problem suffered in the postdivorce period. Discussed are specific ways of working toward new goals and getting what you want out of life. This chapter on behavior control will appeal to those who truly feel lost.

Mitigating the trauma of divorce requires far more than simply bettering one's personal coping and adaptability. It calls for understanding why divorce in America is particularly painful.

First the facts. Who is the typical divorced person? Is he or she the marital nomad who selfishly seeks hedonistic fulfillment? A common everyday person who just can't stand to be miserable anymore? How long does it typically take a person to make and implement the dissolution process? Does the decision to separate physically happen in the heat of an argument or does it evolve over months or years? What are the aspects of a mobile, urban society that will encourage increasing numbers of divorces? Chapter 6, "Facts and Forecast," will enlighten the reader.

Suffering from the label of a nonconformist, the divorced person is surrounded by myths. These myths have done little more than verify the fact that divorce is evil. "Dispelling Myths," Chapter 7, challenges some of these widely-held beliefs:

1. That liberal divorce laws breed marital breakdown.
2. That divorce causes delinquent children.
3. That liberal divorce will undermine the family institution and breed social disorganization.
4. That divorced persons suffer from deeply-rooted psychopathology.

Do other cultures have the same problem with marriages? What ways have they found for dealing with divorce constructively? Do restrictive laws force people to work out their problems? Sweden, Japan, Russia and other nations have been chosen to represent industrialized nations with high divorce rates, but not as high as here, and rehabilitative attitudes towards divorce. Divorces among Eskimos and an African tribe in "Cross Cultural Comparison," Chapter 8, exemplify societies with nearly 100 percent divorce rates. Resources for split partners permeate all of these cultures. The impact of divorce on the individual and society is not nearly as great as it is in the United States.

Compared to other countries, American divorce is especially traumatic. Our ostrichlike insights have only augmented the pain for an individual trying to make some sense out of the experience. The consequences are costly.

Chapter 9, "Why Divorce Is So Painful for Women," describes how our society increases the debilitative aspects of divorce. Hypocrisy among many couples, for instance, tends to be confusing for the person who wonders why marriage is working so well for everyone else. What happens behind the bedroom doors of significant Americans is also discussed in this chapter. The question that is raised is how pervasive, in truth, is our traditional monolithic American marriage? The purpose is not to insult the memory of traditional marriage but to demonstrate that a large segment of our population already has lived out reform.

Inadequate role definition creates excessive and sometimes intolerable ambiguity for the divorced person. "How can I be a better single parent?" "Will my neighbors look down on me for letting my friend stay over last night?" "Would it be wrong for my ex-spouse to become good friends with my new lover?" Few guidelines are provided. The safest place to go from that vacuum is into the well-defined status and role of the remarried. People need some structure to stand on. Improved instruction on ethics and protocol would help.

In the United States, women are particularly crippled by divorce. The women's liberation movement has made great strides in helping divorcees overcome injustices. Impetus for even greater work in that direction stems from the startling statistics provided in Chapter 9 of exactly how unprepared women are for self-sufficiency and independence. Identity-crises for divorced women are particularly common. "What do I *really* want out of life?" "Where do I go from here?" Divorce especially hurts a woman from a traditional marriage. Feelings of inadequacy often propel a dependent woman into the fickle security of remarriage wherein she misses the opportunity that divorce provides to discover herself as a unique individual.

Removing the stigma from divorce does away with societal obstacles blocking the path of the dazed divorced. It restores those "inalienable rights" to life, liberty, and the pursuit of happiness. If couples have irreconcilable differences, they should be allowed to part and find more suitable partners. The powerful forces of affection, love, habit, family, lifestyle, sex and companionship cement marital ties. Without those bonds with which to nurture self and children, individuals deserve the freedom and responsibility to part *without* heavy feelings of failure.

Chapter 10 summarizes the various points made and sketches a blueprint for divorce reform in the United States. This chapter starts with smaller measures we could use to improve the lot of our divorced population and moves on to suggestions for major reform.

Divorce reform begins by helping victims work through the process. Counseling could be made available by the states when an individual files for divorce. The nonlegal aid would supplement the legal process. Researching the area of emotional separation would also help, so that social scientists would have a better grasp of the total problem. Reform is also needed in providing the services which extended families did in previous generations. Important services like child care or services like a place or person to turn to when emotionally upset. Another service could be financial support during an unusually stressful time. Suggestions such as these would go a long way to mitigate the adverse consequences of divorce.

More important, though, is major divorce reform. Trial marriages would truly remove the stigma of divorce. The trial marital contract would last for a specified period of time at the end of which it would be automatically dissolved. The couple would have to renew their own contract and the focus would be on recommitment. Trial marriages would help to avoid divorce. The sequentially married person would not have to live with the societal smudges that breaking a traditional marriage now involves.

Trial marriages would allow for an even greater societal need: pluralism. The one-lane road accommodated the horse and buggy well. Urban areas now employ a whole galaxy of transportation alternatives—bicycle paths, local access roads, alleys, one-way streets, arterials, elevated and depressed freeways, expressways, parkways, superhighways, and bypasses are readily accepted as alternative routes within a city. We need that same pluralism in the ways in which male-female relationships are legalized. Pluralism is the emotional and intellectual acceptance of varied interpersonal contracts. One couple might choose a traditional, exclusive, monogamous marriage in which to conceive and rear children. We need no additional categories to accommodate this traditional marriage. A childless couple may choose to enact a trial run on marriage. While these latter two are common in the 1970s, trial marriage would provide the legal sanction to give these types of relationships society's stamp of approval.

Our one-lane days are over. The casualty list is high for individuals who don't accept the straight and narrow definition of what is acceptable. The suicide rate is inordinately high for divorced men and women. Suicide for a divorced woman is an astonishing 3.5 times more likely than for a married woman according to Hugh Carter and Paul Glick in their book entitled *Marriage and Divorce: A Social and Economic Study.* Suicide for a divorced male is 4.2 times as likely as it is for a married man. One could argue that persons whose mental health would not predispose them to marry or find partners would also be prone to suicide. This would not explain the vast differences between the single and the divorced group.

Death caused by cirrhosis of the liver (linked with alcoholism) reflects another unsuccessful way of recovering from a divorce. The death rate from this for divorced white women was 2.8 as great as it was for married white women, according to Carter and Glick. For divorced white males, the death rate from cirrhosis climbed to over 7.1 times what it was for married white men. We need to take divorce reform seriously.

Pain is mirrored in less dramatic ways. Almost half of the 110 persons contacted in a research project conducted by John Scanzoni entitled, "A Social System Analysis of Dissolved and Existing Marriages," that appeared in the *Journal of Marriage and the Family,* August, 1968, refused to even talk about their experiences. The reason given was that their pain was too great. Another sampling of more than 4000 divorced persons in California by Karen S. Renne, concluded that divorced persons were more likely to report physical disability, chronic illness, neurosis, depression and isolation than married persons. In his large interview survey, William Goode found that 63 percent of the divorced women reported being traumatized by their divorce experience. Other societies don't report this serious a problem, even when they have a high divorce rate.)

The person reading this book who has been through a divorce, or has had friends go through divorce, knows only too well how disruptive it can be. Yet divorce holds out a unique opportunity for self-growth. Full freedom to explore and strengthen assets differentiates marriage from the divorce period. Divorce can be a breaking with the past which allows a new, improved personality to emerge.

Part 1:

"THE STING"
Dissolution Training

Divorce often throws people into a state of limbo. The father suddenly becomes a swinging single. The achievement-oriented person may lose an important area of achievement as a mother or father. A man or woman may find, of necessity, that he or she must work longer hours at domestic and/or paying jobs and has little time for valued hobbies. The person who idealizes being married stands alone. Emotional upheaval often results from this imbalance. This may, in turn, lead to behaviors which are considered dysfunctional by yourself and others and to thoughts which drive you crazy.

While this state of imbalance is a normal stage that most people go through, learning how to cope creatively with it is a relatively unknown art. Psychologists and psychiatrists have been remiss in not educating greater numbers of people about how to gain emotional freedom after divorce.

By emotional freedom, I do not mean a reckless, uncaring or unthinking approach to life. Rather, it involves more self-control in being able to be more or less emotional. Emotional freedom entails being familiar with you own depths of feelings as well as being able to control them. It means being able to let go at will and come out of emotions at will.

If this sounds hard, imagine yourself in a relationship you had so much respect for that you were afraid of it. Wasn't it difficult to let go, to share your inner self, and become dependent? If you became deeply involved, did you find that disentanglement posed great difficulty?

The techniques employed in dissolution training are those I have used with divorcing and divorced persons to mitigate the difficulties of breaking with the past. While you will find a great deal of variety in the methods espoused, you will need to have this at hand for the multi-faceted problems at hand. Dissolution is a complicated process, and I can give no simple remedy for assuaging the pain and heightening the growth. I have included, however, many fundamentals from which you can pick and choose as you find them useful.

The following chapters are designed to impart ways to gain emotional freedom. Few people quietly part as friends and go their separate ways. The evidence already presented points in the other direction: Americans suffer considerably from divorce.

The ways of achieving emotional freedom emerge through three modalities of being: emotions, thoughts and behaviors. Change can begin in any one of these. If behavior changes are made, often the emotions and cognitions catch up to the behavior and help restore equilibrium. For instance, if you have wanted to be more confident in front of people, taking a speech class might raise your confidence level. That behavior (practice in speech class) would change your emotions by making you less tense in front of others and would be likely to change your thoughts about yourself. "Yes, I am capable of delivering a good speech."

Learning how to control your emotions also leads to changing your behaviors and thoughts. Stopping vindictive anger, for instance, eliminates the constant telephone calls to an ex-spouse who doesn't want to be disturbed. Controlling that anger leads to controlling the telephone behavior which leads to more constructive self-evaluations. "Yes, I can control myself and feel better about myself."

The third break-in point, thoughts, exemplifies another angle of change for self-improvement. Change your self-defeating thoughts and your behaviors and emotions change. The thought "I can't stand to live alone" may make you feel anxious and angry. The behavior this thought elicits is sulking. If you decide that, "Yes, I can stand to live alone. Nobody says that having another person around is essential for happiness. I may even find some virtue in being by myself," the mood subsequently changes and behaviors become more active.

Chapter 2 starts with the stages of dissolution. Common stages and feelings are explored. I have tried to point out where negative feelings are helpful to you and when they need to be curtailed. The three subsequent chapters describe how to enhance yourself following divorce.

Chapter 2
Stages of Emotional Divorce

Tormenting and tantalizing. Depriving and stimu-
lating. Lonely and fulfilling. Loving and hateful. Emotional divorce has potential for all of these feelings.

What is the relatively unresearched process of
emotional divorce like? Do people have basically the
same experience in separating themselves from other
loved ones? Are there some predictable patterns?

As was mentioned earlier, more than 839,000
persons divorce every year in the United States. From
1969 to 1973 more than 230 of these divorced persons
have walked into the Georgia State Counseling Center
and requested help in mitigating their problems. Growing through emotional dissolution is a widely experienced, but narrowly researched, mental health concern.
To this writer's knowledge only one book has been
written about emotional divorce, *Creative Divorce* by
Mel Krantzler.

Before writing this book I surveyed many of the
clients who were divorcing or divorced who had come to
Georgia State University Counseling Center during the
early 1970s. The purpose was to ferret out any com-
monalities in the emotional impact of divorce as well as

the stages. The results of the "Emotional Survey of Divorce" are interwoven into this chapter and embellished by clinical experience.

The emotional relationship between two persons usually dies by inches. The stages: (1) disillusionment, (2) erosion, (3) detachment all aim the person toward (4) physical separation. The stage of (5) mourning ensues. Resurrection begins when the person starts feeling the stage of (6) second adolescence. The concluding stage in the process entails (7) hard work. The stages prior to divorce last an average of one and one half to five years. The mourning and rebirth stages vary dramatically in duration and strength.

These stages can be experienced in a much different order than they are presented. Likewise, the duration and intensity of each stage varies according to the individual. Let us trace the evolution of a divorce through its stages.

Disillusionment

Emotional divorce often begins innocently and insidiously. Disillusionment is when you begin to undress the spouse psychologically. One spouse will take off his or her blindfold of romantic involvement and see the real differences.

The shroud of romantic fiction is dropped. Unprepared to deal with the visible differences, the disillusioned spouse often concentrates on the negative. "I just realized that my wife is really sloppy," an angry husband will report. "She leaves her clothes all over the bedroom and bathroom." A frustrated wife inveighs, "He doesn't have the spine to stand up to his parents. He takes money from them and we have to go to visit them every week to pick up the check. I hate it." Another: "I'm living too much in her world, everything I do revolves around her needs."

While these thoughts and statements intrude on the happiest of marriages, prolonged time spent dwelling on them sows the seeds of destruction. At first, awareness of marked differences will slip in and out of consciousness. One moment the partner is the best thing going. The next moment the difference seems intolerable. The evolution involves an increased proportion of time spent in the latter frame of mind.

Disillusionment chips away at the enchantment process. That person who was to fulfill almost all of your expectations, needs and ideals turned out to be depressed, sloppy, a compulsive eater, uninformed, unaffectionate, asocial, domineering, insensitive, uncaring, a flirt, nagging, overly dependent, overly self-sufficient, oversexed or any other characteristic that isn't compatible with your needs. The honeymoon is over. The repetition of occurrences grates on your nerves. You tell yourself at first, quietly, that you shouldn't be irritated; after all, everyone has differences. But the irritation at each instance grows.

When your close friend describes how wonderful his or her marriage is, a dullness overcomes you, as you patiently listen. You agree that your marriage is just fine too, but some of the old assurance is missing in the tone of your voice. At this point, the social team is still very much intact and you may even appear enviable to your friends as a couple. You may both laugh and interact at parties but the private life starts to suffer. The attraction and trust for one another begins to wane. Disappointment feeds itself. Mary, for instance, hungers for a psychologically close intimate relationship with John. She comes home from work excited about a happening she is just dying to tell John about. John isn't home at the expected time and Mary is disappointed. Time elapses and he doesn't call, Finally he comes home and Mary is livid. Instead of sharing her anger and resolving the conflict, Mary buries her feelings, storing both the anger and the excitement inside. Unresolved and cumulative incidents like these are categorized in Mary's mind in the self-fulfilling prophecy of "I don't have the intimate relationship with John that I want."

The disillusionment stage can be helpful when it integrates the expectations of two people with reality. Every spouse needs to go through the process of meshing and differentiating his or her real spouse with the ideal spouse. To the extent that these grievances are openly aired and resolved, the marriage remains healthy. The couple at this stage has the opportunity to rework their contract so as to meet as many of each other's needs as possible while accepting those which they cannot change. Persons who progress on to the next stage, erosion, have stockpiled negative emotions so long that it becomes necessary to purge them (though this usually happens in a rather self-defeating way). The first stage is quite easily reversed if two people are willing and able to admit differences and modify their habits for one another while accepting the unchangeable.

Erosion

《Erosion is the wearing away of marital satisfaction. Although the awareness of dissatisfaction is more conscious at this stage, often the sources are not fully known to the dissatisfied person. If the reasons were known, acknowledged and dealt with maturely and confidently with the other person, the couple would come to terms with the problem and would be happily recycled back to the beginning of these stages. Because so few people have the experience or have developed the skills of intelligently working through differences, this stage is common sequel to the first. Aspirations outstrip abilities.》

Repressed anger and hurt left over from the first

stage, disillusionment, find expression in erosion. Disillusionment can exhibit itself through ulcers, migraine headaches, anxiety, impotence, dysmenorrhea, or heart attacks but very often it manifests itself through an overtly destructive process.

Nonverbal behaviors, verbal responses, and overt behaviors betray the decay. Paul repeatedly gave Joanne his dagger look when they had company for dinner. Joanne learned to interrupt Paul and would contradict the story that he was trying to tell. Arguments are stoked by white-hot words. None of these amounts to much in isolation. Over a period of time, however, cold, prickly nonverbal and verbal behaviors supersede the supportive and warm types.

Unattended and hurt egos kindle the fires of fierce competition. At a social gathering, the two will compete to see how much attention each one can win at the expense of the other. One or both may begin to spend money recklessly. A careful vigilance is maintained to make sure that one does not give any more than the other. The concentration is on taking rather than giving; being loved instead of loving. Both partners feel they are not getting enough.

Avoidance passively erodes. Dick can avoid hearing a request; Paula can avoid doing what Dick asks; Dick can avoid Paula entirely. If Paula breaks down and says that her companionship needs are not being met and could there please be some changes made, the request is met with logical excuses. "I'm sorry, darling, that I had to stay at the office until 11 p.m. tonight. I am doing the best job I can to feed the family and it is vitally important that I finish the project I started on." While the logic of the argument is impeccable, often it runs counter to some basic trust and understanding. Passively resistant to dealing with the problems head on, the avoider confuses the spouse with strong denial that any problems exist. His or her behavior, however, belies that denial.

Disrespect triggers further erosion. Pamela feels that Joel doesn't respect her friends so she, in turn, disrespects his. She doesn't need to say it. She just continues to do the dishes when Joel's friends drop in. The same dynamic can operate with in-laws. The myriad ways that each person can show lack of respect emerge here. Sitting silently at the dinner table for hours with an uninterested expression can be a powerful way of showing your spouse that you don't care to impress his or her in-laws. This disrespect is often retaliation for camouflaged hurt.

Sex turns into a proving ground. The wife or husband can feign a complete lack of interest while the other partner accelerates his or her demands. Sex becomes a battleground with a conqueror and a conquered. The person who is conquered icily endures intercourse. Both lose. Frigidity or impotency during this stage expresses frozen anger.

The interesting thing I have noted in therapy is how many clients think that their spouse doesn't notice their lack of involvement in the process. Women, especially, report they think their husbands have not noticed the fact that they are uninvolved and distanced. They then call their husbands insensitive. What invariably emerges at a later point is the full but nonverbalized awareness of the partner.

Furtive vindictive behavior depicts another covert way of eroding the relationship and expressing anger (right away) and is often rewarded by a comforting extramarital affair. The extramarital affair by itself does not destroy the marriage, however.

What does gnaw at the existing marriage is the guilt of the roving partner. It happens in this way. Beth goes outside the marriage and has her first affair with a man in her church group. At first she is surprised that the sky doesn't fall down on her. She expects to be discovered and isn't. The affair continues. She feels she is deceiving Bob, her husband. She is. She secretly wants to be caught. The logic becomes convoluted and she loses respect for Bob because she can deceive him. Then she asks herself how she could love someone she doesn't respect (sometimes this disguises loss of self-respect).

Her lover meets needs not satisfied by Bob. Beth begins to invest herself emotionally in her lover while putting in ritualistic time with Bob (playing wife). Bob realizes something is awry and cannot put his finger on it. He feels the detachment and yet doesn't want to recognize it. Escalating both his demands for attention and his attempts at patchwork, he futilely extends himself further and further. By definition, he can do very little right at this point. Bonds holding them together become stretched and strained.

Both disillusionment and erosion can be reversed. Disillusionment is easier for a counselor to work with; erosion is a bit harder. Disillusionment stays mostly in the mind. Erosion instills habits that also acquire payoff values. Repetition of putdown behaviors and words engenders a feeling of superiority. Putting the spouse down in front of company brings a rewarding laugh. Forgetting to drop the shirts off at the laundry makes the other person take the responsibility and saves you time. Flirting with friends builds the ego and punishes the jealous mate. Maliciously criticizing a political view allows you to feel one up on him or her. Giving up these payoffs is more difficult than compromising expectations.

The marriage is salvageable during erosion. Despite the destructiveness, the couple are still very much involved with each other. They are still dependent on the flashes of love and prevalence of security that the other provides. Fights may savagely brutalize, but the couple is still fighting. Hurts are deep because the two people still care for each other.

Detachment

Detachment involves a series of emotional deaths. One divorce lawyer in Seattle commented to me when talking about divorce, "If a woman has been beaten repeatedly by her husband and comes in all black and blue, asking for a divorce, the chances are slim that she will follow through with it. If a woman comes in and says she doesn't know what is wrong but that she is bored, the chances are nearly 100 percent that she will return to finalize the papers." If a couple cares enough to fight with each other, the relationship can usually be mended. If a couple feels a low commitment to the relationship, has an eye on the escape hatch, barely shares or talks, avoids physical affection or sex, doesn't look into each other's eyes, very little can be done. Here we find the speechless animosity of mutual disrespect.

The nonverbal manifestations of detachment are blatantly obvious. Eyes are cast down or look past the other person. Bodies are turned away from each other. Arms and legs become locked and symbolically block out the other person. Voices are either harsh and strident or barely audible. Ears don't hear. Jokes fall with a thud to the floor. Faces sullenly mask feelings. Remarks are cursory and succinct, barely answering the question. Each period at the end of the sentence rather than opening up communication, cuts it off. A feeling of tenseness contaminates the air. If expectations are being fulfilled, they are quite often mundane necessities. The emotional plane is arid and barren.

Detachment means you are no longer investing much in the marriage. The underlying feeling is "I don't care." The period is not so much one of intensified conflict as it is an increasing boredom with the conflict. The person finds that the conflict no longer interests him or her. In getting divorced or separated, people escape not so much from the arguments, but from the lack of any purpose, goal or zest left in their resolution. The coldness that was at first withholding of love has become habitual and natural. Empty hulls of people pass each other in routine. Excitement, vitality, investment, enthusiasm, giving, tolerating are all either anesthetized or transferred to another person, hobby, skill, animal or job.

I have seen couples in therapy where only one person has gone through the detachment stage. The prognosis for a person who has been through a prolonged period of deadened emotions is low as far as recommitment to the marriage is concerned. "No matter how hard I work at it, he or she just doesn't pull my chain." "I have tried for nearly a year to have some feelings for him or her; I've lost the battle." Regenerating the love proves nearly impossible.

The tragedy is that many well-intentioned persons start marriage extremely committed to the person and the marriage. They pass through these stages unknowingly and find themselves with deadened emotions that the other can no longer vitalize. By the time the person appears at the counselor's door, little can be done to save the marriage. The wounds are too deep.

Detachment in its full-blown stages involves a switch from a past to a future orientation. The detached person begins to dream of his or her own future—without the spouse. Fantasies of what single life would be like frequently occur. Concrete figuring of the financial gains and losses in being divorced preoccupies the mind. The person often measures his or her appeal to the opposite sex by being attentive to flirtatious glances. Little rehearsals of independence come in the form of insisting on nights out during the week when the spouse does not know one's whereabouts. Often one or the other will go back to school to prepare for a career and to increase financial self-sufficiency. Runaway funds are kept in secret bank accounts.

The thought of divorce may or may not be dominant at this point. Often, the person does not want to give up the security of marriage quite that easily: "We will just try living apart for awhile to see if we can patch up the marriage. Maybe separation will help us get back together." Actually what the person is requesting and needs is time to practice being single with the security of being able to run back into the marriage.

Confusion mounts. To be or not to be single again? As the decision becomes imminent, anger sets in. The person who has been wavering gradually leans to one side: angry separation. Somehow anger makes it easier to decide. Lee paints a very black picture of Mike. The mere thought of Mike's injustices, personality quirks and weaknesses fires her emotions. "I've been used!" "He disgusts me!" "I can't stand the thought of making love to him!" Lee seems to need becoming completely engulfed with hate in order to get out.

Often a person will lurk in the sidelines before the final deciding event. Catching the mate with a close friend precipitates the last-straw feeling of fabricated jealousy. A colossal fight follows. The grand finale: "Now I can get out. I've had it." Oh, were it that simple! While most persons lie in wait for such an excuse, grand finales usually don't terminate the marriage. They do justify separation, though.

The approach-avoidance battle rages. "Do I really have the courage to go it alone?" "Do I really want to go through the loneliness of being single?" "Isn't security better than happiness?" "How do I know that separation will solve my problems?" You seek answers from others. "You see what pain he or she is causing me? I *am* justified in feeling this way, aren't I?"

Physical Separation

You're alone. You've really done it. You are no longer tied to someone else. You are now to face life by yourself. "A little breezy out here in the cold world. Whoops. I wonder if I've made a mistake. My balance is none too good. Maybe marriage wasn't so bad, after all. No, I can't go back now. I've made the decision. I've got to be strong and learn to survive."

Physical separation is the most traumatic aspect of the whole emotional divorce process. Now you have to face loneliness, anxiety, confusion and formation of a new identity. The creative aspects of these states are just barely visible at this point. Feelings in separation vacillate less than when you anticipated living apart. The period of trial divorce has begun.

Betrayed: perhaps you are feeling abandoned. You cling, feeling stunned, and rebuffed. "Come back! I can't stand it. I won't do whatever I was doing wrong. Just please, please come back." Unheard words. The emotional knot tightens. "How can I survive without him or her? What am I going to do? Where do I turn?" The pleas to return fade.

"I've got to face it. I've got to take hold of myself and learn to deal with it. I *can* do it. Oh, if only he or she would come back." Being cut-off brutalizes. You feel betrayed.

A by-product of abandoned loneliness is vigilance. Especially towards the whereabouts of the ex-spouse. One can almost see the same loneliness anxiety repeated in divorce as it was in childhood. John Bowlby, in his recent book entitled *Separation: Anxiety and Anger,* says, ". . . in the presence of a responsive mother figure, an infant or young child is commonly content; and once mobile, is likely to explore his world with confidence and courage. In her absence, by contrast, an infant is likely, sooner or later, to become distressed; and he then responds to all sorts of slightly strange and unexpected situations with acute alarm. Furthermore, when his mother figure is departing or cannot be found, he is likely to take action aimed at detaining her or finding her; and he is anxious until he has achieved his goal." If the mother stays put while the child explores, the result is a contented and curious child. If the mother explores and the child feels abandoned, the result is often a furious, vigilant, defiant youngster. Adults are not much different in marriage separation. The unattached and lonely feeling of separation gives rise to watching carefully how and what the partner is doing.

Lonely thoughts often go hand-in-hand with the hurt. Feelings of inferiority well up and consume the silence. "I feel unloved." "I'll never make it in a relationship." "What do I have that anyone else would want?" The failure cassette is pulled from the memory bank, repeated and repeated and repeated. A certain amount of this helps drain off emotions. Excessive self-flagellation cries out for more professional help.

Initiator vs. *Deserted:* Chances are great that the initiator has worked through the detachment stage prior to separation while the deserted has not. Working through the detachment is a bit easier in the security of partnership. Learning autonomy within the comfort of marriage is like learning to ride a bike with the help of training wheels.

The person who has taken the initiative has a distinct advantage. Even if the dissolution process has been experienced equally by both parties, the person who actually makes the move towards separation and/or divorce preserves his or her own integrity. "I have acted on my (or our) feelings."

The initiator's reactions to separation are no more enviable than those of the deserted. He or she made the decision to separate or file, and often feels guilty about leaving. "I feel that I am no good. I just couldn't stick out the marriage. I hate hurting someone else and I feel that since I made the decision, I hurt him or her. We were mutually miserable but I am the one who decided."

The guilt is even worse if the marriage had been relatively happy. "I just don't understand. Roger and I were basically in love. All of a sudden, I transferred my love to someone else. I just couldn't get back with Roger." That person then chides herself silently, "Maybe I'm a misfit in society. Falling in love with someone else while I'm married should be wrong. But it didn't feel wrong at the time." The person feels guilty about not feeling guilty.

One reaction against the guilt of leaving is to transform feelings into a wall of icy anger. The "I don't have anything to say to you" cold-shoulder reaction to an ex-spouse originates in this camouflage. Harbored and unexpressed irritation ferments into a full-fledged rage by the time of separation.

The initiator has to go through the same expunging process that the abandoned goes through, if the marriage has been at all satisfying. Doubts about the decision are kept quietly in check. If a new lover waits, chances are great that that person will experience the second stage, adolescence, first. When infatuation about the new lover wanes, mourning strikes. Insecurity and fears of loneliness are common to both.

Loneliness. The American way of life nourishes the insidious fears of loneliness. Societal rewards center around conformity, action, acquisition, ambition, imitation, order and predictability. Experiencing aloneness, the unique characteristics of the self and inner motivations conflicts with the attitudes and values of our culture. Being alone with one's self in America represents nothingness, a void, to most people.

Loneliness, with its concomitant guilt and/or abandonment anxiety, does not have to be a negative experience. True, it is intense. Loneliness can also be creative. The depth of feeling generates a bond or sense of fundamental relatedness to others. According to Clark Moustakas in his book *Loneliness,* "Loneliness rather than separating the individual or causing a break or division of self, expands the individual's wholeness, perceptiveness, sensitivity, and humanity. It enables the person to realize human ties and awareness hitherto unknown. . . . In the spiritual and creative experience, there is often no other but the lonely way, perceiving life from one's own being, creating one's self as one wants to be, drawing from one's own resources, capacities, roots. . . . In such experiences, there is often a fixed determination to go one's own way and a courage to stand alone." Out of loneliness comes creativity, strong determination, courage and deep commitment.

Separation Anxieties: Immediately following separations, both parties are likely to come face to face with some intense unexpected emotions. Anxiety is one.

Anxiety is a state of uneasiness and distress about future uncertainties. An anxious person is not anxious about the past or present, but more about the future. Signs of anxiety range from hollow emptiness, to a spaced-out feeling, from restlessness to a near panic. More specific signs are skin sensitivity, rapid speech, feeling a surge of aggressiveness inside, speech disorders, disruptions in thought patterns, omitting words, stuttering, blocking, unnecessary word and sentence repetition and awkward pauses in speech.

The tendency is, when anxious, to overreact. When anxiety becomes too great, you have perceptual problems and cannot perceive stimuli accurately. A person home alone imagines burglars. Shadows pass across the windowpane like dark threats.

Anxiety twists the perception of time. "I go home to an empty house with all those reminders and the loss consumes me. It's awful. The evening stretched over endless darkness. I wanted it to end but sleep would never come." Powerful emotions magnify the internal sense of time. Minutes stretch out to eternities.

Perception is distorted in other ways. What you hear, for instance. You may "hear" a supportive comment from a friend and take it critically. You may find yourself daydreaming excessively. All of the happy memories may be discredited as phony. You may notice a tendency to drink, eat or smoke in order to relax. Endless hours are spent tossing and turning before falling asleep. Nightmares. Fears surface in many ways.

Fear-of-the-Unknown-Anxiety: Anticipation of the unknown in separation is often threatening. The person anticipating being alone worries about meeting financial needs, about being attractive to the opposite sex, about being able to attract another mate, about what parents will think, about the children, about a decline in self-esteem without a partner, about filling companionship needs, and so forth. You worry, "Do I have the courage to handle single life alone? I did it before." Yet the gnawing fear pervades that somehow this singleness is different from the time before you were married. You now have the contrast of marriage to make single life feel emptier.

Breaking-Habits Anxiety: Breaking secure, comfortable habits provides a powerful disruption which breeds feelings of unrest. Few nonpsychologically-minded people realize the tremendous inertia attached to changing a little habit. Brushing the teeth a certain way in the morning, rummaging through your clothes closet, showering and skipping breakfast—all are rituals with which you start the day. Driving down the same road every evening with the same scenery and anticipating the regular dinner allow for predictable, pleasureful events to anticipate. Every day is interwoven with hundreds of these little habit threads. You turn your mind off when repeating a habit and relax. Immediately following separation, these threads are broken. You have to get into a new car pool. You take a different road. You have to take on a second job to support yourself. You can no longer repeat your familiar daily routine into which you settled while married.

Upon separation, the sequence of these behaviors is interrupted and new habits have to be generated to accommodate your new schedule. The uncertainty and lack of practice with new behaviors elicit restlessness and vulnerability. The more mutually interdependent the habits were that the couple had established, the more the individuals are likely to miss them when gone.

You not only have to break those secure old habits but you have to worry about being able to adapt to habits of new people or situations. The anticipation of required adaptability feeds even more frustration into an already vulnerable period.

Identity-Crisis Anxiety: Separation also shakes the self-concept. Allen Wheelis, in *The Quest for Identity,* writes, "Identity is a coherent sense of self. . . . It depends also upon stable values and upon the conviction that one's actions and values are harmoniously related." An identity-crisis occurs when a father, for instance, leaves his family-oriented neighborhood where rearing children is the central value. He enters a swinging-singles apartment. In his new environment, a totally new set of values appears. Exploitation. Making it with the girls. Parties. "It sure looked good in fantasy before divorce. Now I think that I really am a family man." A family man in a swinging-singles apartment? The man has to learn a whole new jargon, a whole new set of behaviors in order to get approval.

One client explained this disruption, "I'm basically a family man. Because I'm divorced though, I have been excommunicated from the neighborhood and the old set of values. My new friends do not fulfill these needs for me. They cannot understand the excitement and joy I experience when playing with my children, or the feeling of accomplishment I feel when Susan brings home a good report card. Yet when I return to the old neighborhood to pick up the children, I feel estranged. An ache rises from my stomach to my throat. I am not really a family man in a family neighborhood anymore. But I am also not the carefree Casanova that my apartment friends would like. I don't fit." This client exemplified the identity-crisis that many separated and divorced persons feel. When basic values and everyday behavior conflict, anxiety results.

Let's take another example of the identity-crisis anxiety. A client, Judy. For nineteen years she devoted herself to her husband and her three children in the traditional wife-mother role. During that time her ideals, behaviors, attitudes and self were externally and internally consistent. A network of like-minded friends reinforced her. Abruptly her husband left her for his secretary. Judy had no coping skills. She had no job skills. She had no identity other than that of wife-mother. She had no friends other than their friends. Developing a career was not congruent with her self-picture. She reported strong anxiety when she was used to being at peace with herself.

If you search through your memory, you will find

that some of those feelings of restlessness were characteristic of your adolescent years. Identity-formation occurs then, too. Trying out new behaviors and not being assured of reinforcement is scary for an adolescent. Learning how to say no to a fellow or girl who has just asked you out for a drink requires practiced confidence. Initiating a friendship you want to pursue takes finesse. The adult already has two strikes: he or she may not be familiar with these new behaviors after being married so long and thinks that at this age one should know them. Results are avoidance, awkwardness and uncertainty. The constructive outcrop of this anxiety is that you are gently nudged into change.

Mourning

The bond is dead. "O.K., I will gather all my strength and bury it." So you reluctantly give your marriage a ritualistic funeral. You tell friends you are splitting. You prepare for life alone. Enter (surprisingly): the ghost of the ex-spouse.

The ghost is much like the memory trace left by an amputated limb. Many persons who have had a leg, for example, amputated in adulthood report they can still feel the sensations from the missing limb. Pain, warmth, pressure perhaps. It is as if the leg is still there reporting back to the brain its state of being. But when he or she looks, the leg is not there.

Memories surround you after separation. The place on the bed where your partner used to be is still almost warm. You want to reach out and touch, but it is only a ghost. You feel a pang of excitement and want to pick up the telephone and call your spouse, but you can't do that anymore.

The stage of mourning helps to purge the former partner from your inner self. Mourning is a web of anger, hurt, loneliness and helplessness. The psychic cleansing is essential. Mourning helps you rid yourself of the ghost. If the process does not happen following separation or divorce, chances are it will appear unexpectedly at a later point in time. I have seen clients who thought they had totally escaped it during divorce only to discover that five years later, they suddenly felt the mourning surge from within and the demand to be dealt with.

Anger: Mourning during divorce unleashes anger. Anger needs a target and will attack anything, but generally heads for familiar territory—the former spouse. The anger appears in irritability, loss of patience, increased rigidity and increased demands. A person with unleashed anger hurls embittered accusations at the ne'er-do-right spouse.

Naturally the angry ex-spouse is not at his or her best. Friends, unfortunately, often do not understand the source of the anger and take it personally. Feeling the divorcing person's hostility, the friend reacts personally and thereby feeds the anger. Understanding that this release of anger is a necessary part of divorce helps to let the person unwind. Just stand back. Let it happen. The anger stage will gradually grow into more compassionate, less irrational, behavior. After a time, the person will decrease his or her dependency demands, not be so irritable, realize that he or she is cared for, is lovable and is a valuable human being. Higher levels of functioning return.

Dysfunctional Anger: The period of getting a divorce tends to be a repetition, as far as anger is concerned, of the marriage. Bitterness in marriage repeats itself through the divorce. Anger, when it does not strengthen, but rather destroys, the bonds between two people, is poison.

Normally anger is a healthy emotional mechanism that serves as a deterrent to disruptive behavior. Venomous anger is no longer "hot displeasure" but rather the malice of hatred.

The vehicle of vengeance is much more sophisticated in divorce than it was in marriage. New levels of escalation are available through lawyers. The stakes are big: custody of the children; property settlement; visitation rights; child support.

This power struggle over the elements of the divorce can torture both partners. Both lose. Each person expends a terrific amount of energy accumulating data for his or her case of being wronged, energy that could be used for constructive growth.

Creative divorce squelches this type of emotion. Persons are still cooperative, understanding and mature about attributing the break-up to irreconcilable differences. Anger as an outgrowth of frustration and hurt is normal. Vengeance desperately exposes unresolved conflicts.

Dysfunctional anger can be a carryover from earlier childhood experiences. Children who experience repeated separations and are constantly subjected to the threat of being abandoned are the most violently angry and dysfunctional of all. John Bowlby in *Separation: Anxiety and Anger* reports studies that children from stable families express distress and concern two to three times less frequently than children from rejecting families. The disturbed children seem to have a history of repeated separations and are much more likely to express anger and/or blame. The residual childhood malice and anger may help determine the degree of blame felt toward the abandoning partner. Counseling helps determine how much of the anger has its roots in the past.

How much energy you put into the relationship before it ended also determines the degree of anger felt. A heavy investment of your emotional, financial or behavioral energies causes the bankruptcy to hurt even more. "Look at all I've put into my marriage. I can't lose all of it now." Yet it is lost. If marriage were the first priority, and one partner poured much of his or her resources into it, the loss of that investment would quite naturally arouse anger. The feeling undergirding the anger, though, is the sense of loss.

Functional Anger: At the same time, anger has a functional value. Anger fills a vacuum created by emotional detachment. "All right, so you no longer care. If I inflict pain, then at least I will be affecting you. If I cannot touch you then maybe I can shock you and force you into passion. Even if I cannot win your love and respect back, at least I can make you feel *something.* I shall make you aware that I am still very much here. See, I am not nonexistent. I can still make your life miserable." Anger is a common way of protecting ourselves from that utterly devastating feeling of total separation. Angry acts insure that the ex-spouse does not entirely cut you out of his or her thoughts. An ugly little spot in his or her mind is better than no spot at all.

Depression: Depression is a sibling of anger. They both involve blame—one inward and the other outward. In depression, the person, instead of blaming another, blames himself or herself. In a constructive sense, depression can be a reaction against the past loss and a preparation for future losses. "I have lost a loved one, a set of friends, the esteem of my family, social approval and something I once enjoyed." Future losses are imminent, too. "I will probably lose some financial security, more comfortable habits and some self-esteem from being rejected." The sadness of depression prepares the person to deal with the losses when they arise in reality.

In our societal avoidance of negative emotions, we

have not developed much tolerance for people who are genuinely depressed. Since we haven't had much experience in helping someone else through it, we try to rush them into cheerfulness. This only makes the situation worse. "Not only am I sad, but Nancy does not accept my sadness. She is uncomfortable with it. Now I've got two people to worry about. I feel worse." Depression is a lonely experience. Having someone close at hand to gently hold the person, or give nonverbal support or just silently to be with the other person is usually all that is needed. The depressed person will come out of it if it is a normal kind of depression. This period is necessary and eventually constructive.

When depression is coupled with guilt, a person denies the mourning by diverting attention from the loss to the enormity of personal guilt. "If only I hadn't demanded so much, my spouse would have stayed." "I shouldn't have kept threatening divorce." "I could have been a more sensitive person." "I wish I wouldn't have to go through this self-defeating routine." Self-accusation ignites anxiety. In pure grief, there is a conspicuous absence of anxiety, since what was feared has in fact happened, and the agitation, anxiety and anger which often occur immediately after bereavement should be regarded as part of the struggle against admitting that the loss has irretrievably taken place. As soon as the sufferer is fully conscious that nothing can be done, despair or deep sorrow takes the place of frantic grief. Irretrievable loss is not frantic, it is just sad.

Second Adolescence

Restoration and Relief: You now feel glad to have made the decision and stuck by it. The conflicts are over. The divorce has at least been decided upon and finalized perhaps at this point. "I am relieved. No longer am I living in hypocrisy. I feel more consistent with myself."

Objectivity about the former spouse and relationship returns to a degree. William Goode concludes that the return to normalcy begins when the individual can look at the ex-spouse and former life with indifference. Instead of looking backward with anger and attraction, the person during restoration and relief is concentrating on personal growth.

Relief: The feeling of relief is difficult to admit for many people going through divorce (much like relief is difficult to acknowledge at the death of someone who has been the source of considerable pain). Our stereotypes have not allowed much room for positive feelings of that nature. Divorce reduces the conflict and pain between two individuals. Divorce frees the person from financial bondage, emotional bondage, and eternal legal commitment. The feeling of having a burden removed prevails. Choices begin to increase. Vision clears. A lighter feeling in not being tied down to someone else feels good. "I'm free!" The excitement of possible new adventures and new risks recreates an almost adolescent state.

Overreaction: Now for the overreaction. No parents to censure. No husband or wife to restrict me. "I think I'll start by sampling the sexual smorgasbord." Previous areas of deprivation whether sexual, travel, fun, hobbies, friends or training often are rigorously pursued. You become sated and fall back into moderation. "I guess sleeping with five different people is not the answer." "Getting involved in all of these hobbies spreads me out a little thin." The imbalance in the opposite direction is gradually replaced by a more comfortable, integrated balance. You discover that dating dozens of different people simultaneously does not fulfill your needs as you once thought it would. Your realize that perhaps you were not caged in by the other person, but rather by your own needs.

Overreaction occurs on another dimension—the clutch. You find a warm, understanding, compassionate person and you want to stay. The other person may not be ready for the extreme dependency you want to transfer onto him or her. You try to restrain yourself but you find yourself getting overinvolved. "I know I have to hold back." But you don't. Soon the other person is skittering off to seek shelter from your over-dependency. Like an adolescent with an unrequited crush, you feel demolished.

Adolescent Trials: The dating game renews old adolescent feelings. "Is he going to call?" "Is she going to accept the invitation?" "I wonder if he will try and seduce me tonight?" "I wonder if she will be willing?" In the sexual pursuit, maturity has added a new variable. The old stereotype of the man always wanting sex and the woman always coyly delaying it has been destroyed. You have learned that the opposite is also true. Men are at a particular handicap in this regard. Say you are not really interested in making love with the girl you are going out with. You do not feel that degree of involvement. How do you tell her that you, as a male, are not interested in sex with her? Only a female can claim virtue. So you say nothing and avoid her. You would like to get better acquainted but are afraid to confront the issue. You might hurt her feelings.

You are exposed to new people. You discover new styles. You have the age and the experience now to know more of what you want out of a partner. Restoration means the return to normalcy and a strengthening because of it. You have reconstructed your personality with both the desirable old parts and some new levels of awareness, maturity, sensitivity and wisdom. The feeling of vulnerability has shaken the once-fixed defense mechanisms enough to reorganize them into a better you. A new confidence in being able to transcend a new experience adds solidarity to the self-esteem. Clients report that they feel more adaptable and more confident as a result of being divorced. You have had to reorder your habits, rethink your goals, restructure your ideals, initiate new friendships and adapt to new people. The anxiety that originally plagued you about whether you could do all these things is now behind you. You have passed the test of self sufficiency.

Exploration and Hard Work

With renewed vitality, you begin earnestly to pursue your self-chosen goals. The state of anxious floundering is over and the recommitment to life and goals ensues. Instead of seeing overwhelming, unreachable future aspirations, you have broken down the dreams into manageable, reachable units. You implement a plan of action. You are self-rewarded and rewarded by others for accomplishment. A new intimate relationship, a commitment towards the children, a series of successes on the job.

You are now ready for a relationship not out of weakness but out of you own strength. You feel the desire and have better tools with which to enter an intimate relationship without debilitating fears of failure. Readjusting to the habits of a new person, getting to know his or her likes and dislikes, gaining new knowledge about another human being on an intimate level becomes an exciting challenge. New insights into self and others encourage additional investigation and inquiry.

The activity in these stages has usually shifted from passive to active. Instead of being acted upon, you become an actor. As an actor you are able to control your own destiny more capably and also have a greater impact on people with renewed self-confidence, a strengthened identity, a greater ability to take risks.

The last stage does not happen in isolation. By this time, other significant persons are intimately involved. You are more approachable and better able to receive kindness and compliments. In turn, you are giving more. Reinvestment in a job may have already reimbursed you with higher pay, more attention or a promotion. Feedback from the outside enhances your internal feelings of worth. Now at the end of the divorce process, you have changed from being stymied to being strengthened by it.

Summary

As mentioned previously, each person going through the emotional disentanglement process will feel any of these particular stages to a greater or lesser degree. Likewise, any one day in the life of a divorced person may involve several stages. Counseling helps those who are blinded by emotions and need help in monitoring the process.

No one is ever totally divorced from a person once truly loved. Fond memories, pleasant times together, unique personality traits of the other, never totally fade away. Being able to cope with both painful and pleasant memories is part of a creative emotional divorce.

Chapter 3

Emotional Freedom

Separation Pathos

"I want to scream! I feel left in the dust, as if my partner took off down the road. There I am. Left. Last night I tried to sleep. I knew I had to clear my mind. But, how? I forced it. Twenty minutes later I was walking the floor."

"Why?" I kept asking myself. "I don't understand. We had a beautiful relationship. We watched our friends' marriages crumble all around us. We thought we really had it licked. How could this happen to us?"

"If only I weren't being treated so cold and indifferent. It is almost like an about-face. One minute we were going to be friends, no matter what. Now he (she) couldn't care less. Love for me must have been dead for a long, long time."

"I feel crushed. Five years of marriage. A major hunk of me is just torn out. I can't believe the cold and uncaring looks. Three days ago we planned *everything* together. Now suddenly I'm left alone." These are the pained words of clients separated less than a month.

Separation often torments. You alternate periods of being a scream machine, feeling empty, numb, and deeply regretful—all thrown into one bag, separated only by minutes. Only time makes sense out of the immediate pathos of separation.

Later those feelings are separated by hours, then days. Labor pains of divorce take anywhere from two months to years. Normally you'll just have to expect them to run their course. Eventually, the emotions die. If you need to develop the capacity to rescue yourself from your own emotional undertow, continue reading.

Emotional Freedom

The end goal is freeing yourself from a long-lasting, emotional bondage. Emotional freedom does not mean freedom from emotions. It does not mean self-deception, phoniness, aloofness, unfeelingness or lack of involvement. Emotional freedom means being vital emotionally, being able to feel and show one's true emotions. It means being able to commandeer your own spirits when you need to. Emotional freedom releases you from being imprisoned by your own emotionality.

How? You need to be aware of when to snap out of your anger, when to step out of your depression and how to moderate your own anxiety. Chapter 2 explored the healthy and productive aspects of these emotions. Anger, depression, helplessness and anxiety are necessary ingredients to emotional divorce. The best advice is to see what you can discover in the pathos. The depth of feelings uncovers unexplored parts of you which enable creative awareness and change. Don't fight the feelings, ride with the current of emotions instead of trying to swim upstream. If you find, however, you need to alter your course and moderate your consuming anxiety, depression or anger, read on.

Do-It-Yourself Emotional First Aid

Anxiety: Anxiety in divorce is a robber of happiness. Unless you are one of those people who are calm and casual, no matter what the catastrophe, you will run into episodes of anxiety during pre- and postdivorce periods. You will find yourself restless, nervous, irritable, scared and sleepless for short spurts from time to time.

Mild anxiety is tolerable. We usually let it run its course and know that the end will come. Other persons find that they have little tolerance or control over tension-filled anxiety. They want to crawl out of their skins and run away from themselves.

At the end of the continuum, anxiety is like an empty feeling in the pit of the stomach, tightness in the chest, panic, a quavering voice, a feeling of pending doom. You feel vague apprehension without recognizing the source.

Diffuse anxiety necessitates psychological therapy and sometimes temporary medication. Some kinds of anxiety can be helped by a technique known as systematic desensitization.

Anxiety Reduction: What if you are recently divorced and are afraid of developing friendships with the opposite sex? You don't experience much trouble after the first ten minutes of talking. The first ten minutes, though, are dynamite. Your anxiety plugs you up so that you trip over your words, awkwardly ramble on and hardly know what to do with your hands. You constantly keep a TV camera in your mind monitoring your potential failure. You flub. You stumble. Confidence dips to a low ebb.

Oh, to learn to relax during those moments! To

have command over your body so that it will be confident when you want it to! Anxiety reduction offers a method whereupon, with practice, you can regulate your own anxiety.

Relaxation and anxiety do not simultaneously co-exist in the same organ. Your heart, lungs and muscles cannot be tense and relaxed at the same time.

Most of us are familiar with the feeling of anxiety mounting. We can feel the heart start to palpitate, the breathing begins to accelerate, and underarms start to sweat. Our speech quickens and our movements become jerkier. Anxiety reduction helps you learn how to put the brakes on those feelings and replace them with feelings of warmth and softness.

Learning anxiety reduction requires a trained person to oversee and guide you through the process for awhile.

Instruction about how to relax has been revamped in recent times by several psychologists, but essentially remains similar to Edmund Jacobson's training (1938). Jacobson is credited with developing the technique of progressive relaxation. Approximately ten sessions in the office and several fifteen-minute sessions at home enable a person to practice the art of relaxation.

The process involves lying prone in a darkened room. The guide should have a soft monotonous voice to help lull you as he or she instructs. The guide first tells you to concentrate on breathing deeply. Breaths are taken from way down in the diaphragm. The stomach is contracted during inhaling and released during exhaling. Then you are asked to tighten the muscles slowly in the right hand. The tightened fist is held about five to ten seconds with as much tension as possible. Then you are asked to notice the difference in the sensations between the tense and the relaxed state. You are encouraged to let the hand relax more.

The same instruction is repeated in many different ways for the left hand, the right and left forearms, the upper arms, the right and left feet, right and left calves, etc. Each part of the body is encouraged to relax and feel warm and heavy. The hypnotic effect of this progressive relaxation is to eliminate all signs of anxiety in the body. The muscles should end up perfectly relaxed.

By working with the separate muscle groups, you learn to differentiate where tension starts to arise in your body. Some persons feel it first in the shoulders, some in the jaws, some in the legs, some in the neck, some in the stomach, some in the back. With greater awareness of when tension begins, you learn to recognize it early and halt it. You have trained your muscles so you can self-instruct them to relax on demand.

Direct control over that feeling of getting uptight is an asset that is portable and functional in a multitude of settings. Taking a test. Giving a speech. Meeting an important person. Asking for a date.

Psychologists and psychiatrists take this progressive relaxation process one step further in working on specific phobias by using imagery. The process is called systematic desensitization. Take the original example of being afraid the first ten minutes with a stranger. You quiver and quake at the mere thought.

First, you run through the process of progressive relaxation. You couple this eased autonomic state with a series of anxiety-provoking images. The images are arranged in the order from least anxiety-provoking to most anxiety-provoking. What systematic desensitization amounts to is mentally practicing the once nerve-racking event with a relaxed body. The process tends to diffuse the event for you. This imagery that has become desensitized carries over into the real life situation and you find yourself more comfortable in those previously anxiety-provoking settings.

While this process is not dangerous to try independently, it can be frustrating. You need someone to help you learn the process of relaxation as well as help to develop your own hierarchy. Once you have the guided instruction, you can apply it on other areas of tension.

Training in progressive relaxation and systematic desensitization is available through many private psychologists and psychiatrists, many college counseling centers and many community mental health centers.

Yoga: One other means of directly controlling what is going on inside the body is found in yoga. Yoga is too complicated to explain within the confines of this treatise, but it essentially involves suppressing body and mental activity. Both can induce a quieting effect. The quieting effect of yoga is particularly helpful with those persons who are predisposed to anxiety attacks.

Yoga classes are offered through most urban YMCAs or YWCAs, as well as noncredit evening classes on college campuses.

Depression

(While depressions are normal and often constructive in all of us, they sometimes pass into the dysfunctional zone. Marital separation is a time of heightened emotionality which means that depression, too, may get out of control.)

The following symptoms signify that the depression needs to be reversed: any little obstacle bogs you down, your sluggish body drags through the day, thoughts run in endless circles through you mind. Often there will be a preoccupation with bodily functions. Day after day after day.

Synthetic Motivation: (1) Set up a strict schedule for yourself. Pepper the routine with activities which you enjoy (even if you are presently putting in a ritualistic time until your capacity to enjoy increases). Often I will schedule a depressed client at 9 a.m. just to make sure he or she gets out of bed. Force yourself into commitments with friends, relatives, a job or anyone.

Passive activities sometimes provide the integral step on the road to recovery. Movies. Plays. Lectures. A stroll through the park. Activities which you can attend with a friend which create an oasis of tranquility but do not force you to take on more than you can handle. At the first sign of relief, increase the activity level and get involved.

(2) Educate your friends. You may have to teach your friends how best to handle your depression. Just being with you or offering silent nonverbal support is really all that is necessary. One depressed client enjoyed having her friend sit beside her while both read.

Agreeing with your irrational thoughts will not help you out of depression. Unless you are working through an exploratory depression (where you get into your feelings, become aware of them and gradually ascend), discourage your friends from helping you drown in your emotions.

The same is true for crying. Crying is a helpful emotional outlet which is a natural expression in experiencing loss. A supportive shoulder may be all that you need to release your emotions during this time.

Hysterical outbursts of crying continued over and over, self-abuse or extreme agitation can feed on itself. When that happens advise your friends to take some authority in stopping you. How? A firm tone of voice telling you to shape up. A firm grip on your shoulders forces you to look your friend directly in the eyes. Either will help startle you out of the wallowing.

(3) Indulge rather than neglect yourself. Poor grooming often accompanies depression. Neglected hair, cleanliness, attention to clothes all reflect downward

spiral. Catch yourself at the first signs of this and force yourself to indulge yourself.

One good way of helping mollify depression is to pursue temporarily your now muted dreams. Sit down by yourself and think of those things or goals that you would really like to have. Just for awhile put aside self-deprivation thoughts with which you usually abort your dream. "I can't afford it." "I don't have time." "It would be irresponsible." Choose just one or two things that you would really like to do, if you would allow yourself to pursue that fantasy. Then start planning.

I am not advocating unbridled hedonism here. In depression you are usually not capable of it anyway. Most of us put off many dreams that are attainable with the excuse that we need to be more responsible. Responsibility in the postdivorce period is heavy enough. The period of postdivorce is a good time to pursue purposely pleasureful activities and dreams.

You can go back to austerity later when the rest of your life is restabilized.

One client, for instance, disappeared into his music. He upped his piano lessons from one to two sessions a week and engulfed himself in this love. Another client had wanted to be a pilot for as long as he could remember. An early marriage and three subsequent children ate up his salary so as to prohibit even thinking about flying. Divorce further pinned him against the wall financially. He needed something, though, to look forward to. Borrowing a little from the car account, a little from the food and entertainment funds and planning frugally, he was able to assemble enough money to finance flying lessons. This hobby gave him the necessary boost when he was headed downward. Having that hope to pull out of the spin helped to lift him out of a destructive depression.

Betray your own Judas: The Judas side of your personality will probably try to undercut your uplift program. Cancelling out on commitments. Sneaking in excessive irrationality on sympathetic friends. Withdrawing from your dreams.

(1) Self-control. Keep control. Play tricks on your Judas by setting up activities which you will have a hard time copping out on. Choose friends who are strong enough to maintain their own sense of self when you want to pull them into the quagmire.

(2) Thought control. You have just come home from a movie with a friend. But you still have the rest of the night to face alone. That ugly obsession which plagued you before you left returns. And you thought the temporary relief would be more permanent!

You need to work on thought stopping. If distractions don't work, then force yourself to take other measures. One method which has worked for many is to write out your thoughts. Sit down with pen and paper and write out every thought you are having. If it is the same thought over and over again, repeat the sentence on paper. When you arrive at the point where you cannot stand to see another repetition of the same sequence, you will stop.

In conclusion, depression, within limits, is a sincere expression of loss. It touches a deep inner core that often exposes new insights. Fighting moderate depression may only make it reappear at a later date. The best idea for this kind of depression is to let it run its course.

Poisonous depression can be modified by deliberate attempts at buoyed spirits. While at first it will feel like you are acting, gradually the mood catches up to the behavior. Only mind can move mind—and the difference is within you.

If emotional resurrection does not happen after a

prolonged period of time, then psychotherapy is strongly advised.

Anger

Anger is a secondary emotion. It is generally a reaction to feelings of loss, fear, helplessness, victimization and/or guilt. Consider your reaction to the driver who dangerously darts in front of you on the freeway. You might utter a few hot words under your breath in an expression of anger.

Actually, the anger came second. First you felt afraid for possible physical damage that might have been done if he hit you. Or perhaps a premature sense of loss that your car might be dented. Your secondary reaction was anger.

So it is in divorce. Use your anger to help you get in touch with what the primary feeling was. Hostility can be an excuse for failure.

Jerry, a thirty-two-year-old graduate student, got a divorce immediately after he graduated from his Master's degree program. His wife, Barbara, had financed his entire education. She felt exceedingly angry at the fact that she had invested her money in augmenting Jerry's earning capability. Upon divorce, she was left to scratch up enough money to put herself through a Master's degree program that she had reluctantly put off.

Underneath the anger lay a feeling of being used. Furthermore, she was disgusted with herself for not taking care of herself during marriage. When she recognized the responsibility she had in the process, her anger mellowed.

Selflessness is a slippery topic. Barbara wanted to sacrifice and give to Jerry during his time of need. In return she expected the same when he completed his program. Therein lay the source of anger. She had put out this terrifically delicious and valuable bait hoping to be rewarded by a fish, but the fish got away. *With* her bait.

Giving entails lots of risk. When we lose, we tend to forget about the original risk and blame the other person for not coming through. Anger releases some of the frustration inherent in not receiving "our due."

In summary, make sure that in life you are not setting yourself up for a letdown. If you have already done so, you can take the piercing edge off your anger by recognizing your responsibility in how you were exploited or rejected or abandoned. You may not be able to retrieve your loss from this relationship, but at least you can help prevent it from happening in the future.

Divorce Counseling

If you are stuck on an emotional plane with no place to turn, I highly recommend counseling. Divorce counseling is for the individual or couple who wants an enriching divorce, one where both individuals become stronger for the experience. What, you may ask, are the benefits of divorce counseling? Why should people work on something they have already decided to end? Isn't that like kicking a dead horse?

Emotional divorce is painful for both persons. Counseling provides an ongoing neutral outsider to help point out how to lessen the pain. Divorce counseling promotes lessening of emotional tension, clear thinking, training and increased sensitivity.

Emotional Drainage: One of the most desperate needs of those going through a divorce period is a person or place to siphon off those strong feelings, a place to vent anger, guilt, hurt, worry and relief. Where could you go?

Friends are the number one resource for those

having emotional difficulties. While friends provide an invaluable refuge for the distraught person, they frequently cannot absorb the total burden. Friendships are normally reciprocal communication and sharing flows in a back-and-forth pattern. During divorce, the pattern is disrupted for the person weighted down by the experience. He or she needs to take in a unilateral fashion from the friendship, needs to be listened to, empathized with and supported. Friendships can endure temporary one-sidedness, but tend to wither if the one-sidedness is excessive and prolonged.

Preoccupation with self is a natural by-product of heightened emotionality. Counseling accommodates one-sidedness without future repercussions (losing your friends). You can then either take a temporary "time out" from your friendships until you begin to restore harmony or at least be a little less of a drain on them.

A friend is a valuable asset to have when you need one. Be sensitive to how much you are using friends as therapists and how they feel about it. If you find yourself abusing friendships, get yourself a counselor.

Using a sympathetic friend can be frustrating to you if you really need counseling. While the well-intentioned ear patiently listens to the worries and anger, the owner of the ear often doesn't know how to provide effective therapy. Frustrated by the feeling that he or she is not doing any good, your friend finds the rambling tiresome and shows it. You then feel hurt because you have opened up and the friend cut you off. You retire deeper into yourself.

Clarification: One of the most painful aspects of divorce is ambiguity. "Why was I rejected?" "Why did I lose my feelings for him or her?" "Could I have done anything which would have kept us together?" The reason many give for marital breakdown is often not the real reason.

Most Americans, for instance, lack skills in dealing with confrontation and honesty within an intimate relationship. "I didn't want to hurt him or her." So instead of correcting the irksome characteristic, the spouse lets the resentment grow and grow and grow. The resentment soon spills over into other areas. The picture becomes clouded with unexpected anger, and the love slips away. The stated cause of divorce might be that the wife drank too much or the husband worked too late. But the problem had its roots in many other hidden disparities.

Counseling can help two individuals to look at the origins and consequences of individual differences. Myra, for instance, may have a hidden desire to fail so that nothing in her life is destined to succeed, including the marriage. At every available opportunity, Myra sabotaged the togetherness of the relationship. Her husband, Phil, did not recognize what was making her so unhappy. He tried and tried but nothing worked. Phil was exhausted and Myra felt frustrated. The origins of this marital problem may have been found in Myra's upbringing, in which case therapy or counseling would have helped her develop a realistic way to change that defeating pattern. Both needed to understand the source of her self-defeating behavior. Phil could have been reinforcing it unknowingly by futilely trying to run circles around the problem. Myra would have to make up her mind that she would give up the unsatisfactory script and grow into a more constructive, successful person. Phil could help reinforce her decision.

Behaviors become systematized. Unsatisfactory marriages tend to polarize people. David starts out with a nucleus of feeling deprived (predisposition from childhood) and slowly the feeling grows stronger. He begins to gather data from the marriage that Elaine is also depriving him of love. Since Elaine is being accused of depriving, she reacts to the accusation by withholding more.

David intones: "You neglect me. You never listen to my long stories. You always go off in your own world reading your books." Elaine doesn't appreciate the anger, so she disappears deeper into her books as a way of punishing David for the anger. David has not considered his part in setting up the polarization. He may be negatively reinforcing Elaine every time she does try to listen. His demands may be more than Elaine wants to satisfy. Elaine has not dealt with her anger about being disrespectfully dealt with. She stores the anger and expresses it passively by not listening. Both need to change the process of negotiating the problem. Counseling helps clarify what the real issues are.

The importance of this cannot be overemphasized. Problems that really break up marriages are most often the ones not reported. Drinking, physical abuse, too much travel, affairs and communication problems are standard categories into which reasons for divorce are lumped. These pat answers help ward off family and friends. Actually, many couples who are getting a divorce honestly don't know why. They have some vague, unspoken feelings about being intensely dissatisfied but each does not know why.

A trained eye and ear can spot patterns. Hundreds of little patterns can abusively perforate a marital relationship. The counselor helps the couple recognize what patterns are unique to their relationship. The purpose is not so much to save the marriage but to make it a learning experience for the couple. If they want to reunite, more power to them.

The point is that regardless of whether the couple continues to divorce or decides to reunite, clarification assuages some of the pain. Each person can walk away with a fuller understanding of self-dynamics as well as how the partner interacted with those dynamics.

Taking partial responsibility for what has happened to you often is made easier through counseling. One client, for instance, came into the counseling center and said that her husband had left her. When asked what the counseling center could do for her she replied, "Get my husband back!" I explained to her that we were not trained kidnappers but that we could help her work through the process.

Her husband did return long enough for divorce counseling. While she had totally absolved herself of responsibility of wrongdoing, she had consistently denied her suffocating demands. The little girl in her placed inordinate requirements on her husband. He had to be home exactly at six. He could not talk to any other females at a party. He had constantly to reassure her that he loved her, and still she wouldn't believe it.

Meanwhile, she painted herself as the perfect wife. She faithfully and laboriously had dinner ready at exactly six. She compulsively kept the house clean. She satisfied the two children's every need. She felt that she was playing out the part of the wife and mother perfectly. She was, to the exclusion of spontaneity and freedom.

She used the image of the perfect wife-mother to justify her insatiable demands. Her identity was totally lost in the role. As she committed herself more completely, she demanded more in return.

Actually, her emotionality and frustration suffocated her in the end. Counseling helped her recognize that she had not been attending to herself. She needed to get out of the selfless-martyr role and pay attention to her own self-satisfaction. As long as she was living through the other members of her family, she was killing everyone, including herself, with kindness. Finding other ways of fulfilling her needs took the pressure off the family to do so.

Take another instance of denial. Peter, a twenty-seven-year-old architect, said, "My wife is unreal. She runs off with her girl friends on nights I am home. I know she has gone to bed with my best friend. Sometimes she doesn't come home from her nightly escapades until three or four in the morning. I'm fed up."

Further elaboration detailed a whole series of instances where the husband had been brutalized. The wife emerged as an insensitive, uncaring nymph. The wife confessed that she did not believe in monogamy, needed some security in marriage, but did indeed pursue outside romances.

What therapy uncovered was the fact that this husband was attracted to women who roam. He acted like a rock himself but chose a woman who pushed the limits. He knew that she was like this before they married but decided to involve himself anyway. The constant turmoil was exciting to him. A reliable, faithful woman would have been boring. He had created his own dilemma.

Sources of Imbalance: To detail the myriad patterns, origins, consequences and processes of marriage breakdown and divorce is beyond the scope of this book. The intricate network of family interaction is, likewise, unique to each family. For this reason I suggest counseling if you are confused about the dynamics of what is or was happening.

I have, however, noticed three areas which generate imbalance in a marriage. Consider them signs which should encourage you into exploration.

(1) Considering the marriage as an end rather than a means. One or both of the spouses consider the marriage static rather than dynamic. "Boy, after I'm married, I can really relax! No more having to worry about courting! No more having to figure out what he

or she is trying to say! I won't have to compromise or give in to his or her wishes." After marriage, the two do indeed relax. A year elapses and they take each other for granted. Each spouse feels that he or she knows the history, nuances, foibles and strengths of the other well enough to consider the learning process done.

"Whew. I can graduate from that hard task and now get to work on some things I have been neglecting. I'll focus on my job for awhile."

Each partner's feelings, demands, expectations, attitudes and patterns of relating are, however, in a constant state of flux. The result of taking a partner for granted, and feeling that you thoroughly know him or her, is called marital drifting. One person within a system cannot change without changing the whole system. An imbalance follows. If the imbalance is ignored or is not corrected for, tensions build.

Example: the football widow. Betty marries Wilson because both are madly in love and need each other desperately. Betty and Wilson are shy socially so they both don't have many contacts with the outside world. During their courtship, they enjoyed attending local football games and spending Sundays snuggled in front of the network football game. Betty's shyness dropped away after two years of marriage and she became more social. She cultivated a couple of female friends and started playing bridge. That led to invitations out to dinner with the husband and wife team of her bridge partner. Wilson said no. He continued to watch football. Betty branched out and developed some male friends.

Soon the passivity of her husband began to bother her. She became more and more receptive to the advances of one of her male friends. By the time Betty realized that marriage is a meshing of two ever-changing people, she was somersaulting in an affair. She had already transferred her feelings to the new lover.

Emotional Freedom

Drifting can be reversed, if it is caught in time. One must first realize that each little imbalance needs to be resolved close to the time when it first appears. Satisfaction is not going to come after the end of the football season, it needs to be happening during it, too.

Another example of this is the comment I hear frequently from the wife or husband of a student. "When Katherine gets out, everything will be perfect. I am miserable now. I can hardly wait until this ordeal is over. I am willing to put off my happiness until she gets through but I am really getting impatient for that to happen," bemoans martyred Ron. Ron tolerates all of the irritating processes, all of the neglect, all of the unfulfilled needs. Ron's happiness hinges on graduation day. Graduation day comes. Nothing really changes. Unhappiness has become ingrained in his expectations and systematized in their interaction. The marriage fractures. Ron feels cheated, frustrated, used and deprived.

Neglect any relationship and it will atrophy.

(2) Lack of a mutual definition of love. What, exactly, are the ingredients of love? One spouse may jumble the affection and warmth usually noted in love with other resources, such as services, goods, money or status. For the other spouse love stands alone. Let's consider some examples where definitions of love differ for two people.

Goods and love: Popular in our materialistic culture, this combination is losing popularity. Women were particularly vulnerable to this lack of differentiation.

Love was defined according to how much the partner gave you in material goods. Dot, for instance, would scrutinize her Christmas present. To her, the worth of it was a barometer of her husband's affection. It was a mink coat in 1965. She felt particularly loved. The next year when it was a watch, she spent three months worrying.

One common translation of this is the silent demand, "If you love me, you will provide for me." Men, too, get caught in this trap. Mark's self-esteem, for instance, was determined by how much he could buy for his family. When he lost his executive job making $40,000 a year and had to scrounge for another, he felt totally worthless as a husband and a father. He had a difficult time receiving love for the six months he was unemployed because he felt he was not giving any.

Services and love: Mary defines love as both affection and services. When Mary was a little girl she was exposed to undifferentiated love and service. Milk and warmth flowed from her mother's body simultaneously. Mary's helplessness made it mandatory to combine both.

As Mary matured and learned how to feed herself her mother could give or deny that service. Service could be used as a bribe in expressing love. "If I didn't love you, I wouldn't drive you to school every day."

Conversely, at a later date Mary can withhold services from her mother. Mother indirectly cajoles, "If you love me, Mary, you will clean up your room." Mary responds and proves her love to her mother.

Service and love for Mary are fused. Mary hardly realized that when she married George. In George's family, love stood by itself. He gave and received warmth and affection—without any service hookers. Mary now assesses George's feelings for her by how many little errands he runs.

"If he loved me, he would automatically help clear off the table and help with the dishes," laments Mary. "I appreciate his telling me that he cares and showing me by constant affection. That doesn't make up for his not trying to make my life easier."

George and Mary are at loggerheads. He feels angered that his messages of love are not getting through. He cannot understand why Mary is putting so much stock in him helping around the house. George and Mary need to respect this basic difference and learn to deal with it.

Status and love: (a) Let's take another case where the differentiation between status and love is present in one partner and not in the other. Barbara and Tim. Tim was taught as a child to respect his father and mother. He was punished for arguing with them, disagreeing with them or expressing his own opinion counter to theirs. Love was withheld any time that Tim showed disrespect to his parents, his parents' friends or to any authority figure. In his mind, being contradicted was equivalent to being unloved.

Barbara came from a family where status and love were clearly differentiated. If you had an opinion, you voiced it loudly and firmly. Contradiction did not subtract from the love you felt.

Election time rolls around. Barbara and Tim engage in a political discussion in which Barbara wholeheartedly bludgeons Tim's argument. Tim's tension builds and he feels rejected. For Tim, if you attack his ideas, you don't love and respect him.

(b) Status can become confused with love in an achievement-oriented person, also. Bill was richly glorified for achieving good grades in early years. His father praised him earnestly when he did a good job repairing the family car. Bill was richly glorified for achieving good grades in high school. Love from parents abounded whenever Bill achieved. When Bill married, he chose Patricia, a public relations writer. Patricia had achieved public acclaim for her skills in news editing.

Patricia got fed up with the high pressure of her job and quit. Bill felt guilty about losing respect for his wife. He began to nag her about joining another news staff and recapturing her fame.

For Bill, love was an alloy of status and tenderness. Respect for Patricia undergirded his love for her. When she stopped achieving, Bill stopped loving.

Patricia could not understand the sudden marital funeral dirge. Her love for Bill was independent of status and she perceived the same in reverse.

Summary: Imbalance results from the lack of a mutual definition of love. Recognizing and dealing with it helps take the tension out of the imbalance.

(3) Lack of skills in conflict resolution. American society, until recently, emphasized control, conformity, rational thinking and, above all, achievement. The power of feelings was vastly underrated. A woman was allowed a meager amount of feeling hurt and being used. For the most part she was expected to be loving, cheerful, sacrificing and selfless. Men could express anger but had to inhibit feelings of hurt. The quintessence of being a man was to have no feelings at all.

Inhibition of feelings oiled the machinery of the traditional-role marriage. Success in this kind of marriage was based on whether or not persons performed their respective duties. Personal intimacy and sharing were not expected. Feelings interfered with a strict task relationship.

Times have changed. Psychological intimacy is now extolled. Gates have been opened for the expression of real feelings in marriage. Anger. Pride. Hurt. Joy. Eroticism. Anxiety. Tenderness. Jealousy. Cautiousness. Excitement. Depression. Positive feelings are pretty easy for most of us to handle. Negative feelings (especially in a mate) are not.

How and when do you help the partner ferret out real feelings instead of trying to distract him or her? How can you help someone through depression? What can you do when your love is so nervous he or she can't sit still? What will move him or her over to one side of the fence or the other when that person is sitting in the middle of a decision for too long?

Helping the spouse work through an emotional problem extraneous to you poses less of a threat than an argument. Anger directed at you is another story. In one case you had the satisfaction of feeling that you were at least trying to help. Frontal attacks threaten you and your personality directly.

It is difficult both to give and receive anger in marriage, for two reasons. First, something desirable (your relationship) is at stake. You don't want to express anger because you are afraid you will hurt the spouse and therefore encourage him or her to retaliate. Being the object of someone's anger poses a threat because you may have to change.

The second common problem is found in not knowing the difference between constructive and destructive anger. What are the rules of fair fighting? When do I give full vent to my grievance and when do I postpone it? What are fair topics for contention and which are foul? Which differences between us are irreconcilable and which are changeable? How do I learn to cope with irreconcilable differences? How can I get my anger out yet make the outcome constructive?

If you are interested in differentiating destructive from constructive anger, *The Intimate Enemy* by Dr. George Bach provides insights. Beyond that I suggest counseling.

Summary: Negative emotions can be transformed from feared failure experiences to friends and helpers with desire to learn and proper training. Otherwise stored anger interferes with marital success.

Sensitivity Training: Divorce counseling enables the two individuals to be more aware of themselves and more aware of the partner. Much of this is subtlety training.

Verbal communication whispers. Nonverbal communication yells. Many persons are unaware of their own body language.

Systems of nonverbal interaction after a few months of marriage ossify. Little behaviors like quick nods, twinkling eyes, critical glances, rigid posturing, avoidance of eye contact, locked arms, tone of voice, rapidness of speech, hesitation, spatial distancing. Thousands of delicate repetitions communicate your relationship with your spouse. Respect, love, esteem, affection, warmth, freedoms, constrictions, all flow primarily through nonverbal channels. Raising your awareness can happen in divorce counseling. You can then take the higher consciousness and transfer it to new friendships.

Divorce Training: The same values which make a good marriage make a good divorce. Trust. Honesty. Cooperation. Communication. Fairness. Emerging from divorce as your ex-spouse's friend is the ultimate goal.

One divorce fiction in our society promulgates that you should be completely in, or completely out of, the marriage. The process of divorce accents the final division: lawyers often perpetuate the myth by advising the originally cooperative client to be hard-nosed and greedy. While deciding on divorce the couple is rational, just and mutually supportive. By the end of the property settlement, child custody decisions and legal process the couple tears at each other's throats.

Summary:

The chapter described a number of ways to regain emotional freedom after divorce. The first method presented was a do-it-yourself emotional first aid technique where you used your anxiety, depression and anger to gain deeper awareness of yourself and others. Inherent were tips on how to reverse these feelings when they lasted too long or became too debilitating.

The benefits of divorce counseling as a way to gain emotional freedom were subsequently spelled out. Emotional drainage, clarification, sensitivity training, and divorce training: all vital pain-reducing components of divorce counseling. Dragging a heavy past around is something few people aspire to. Both the individual first aid and divorce counseling help to untie that emotional knot—if that is what it has become—binding you to someone you do, or once did, love.

Chapter 4
Purging Demons from the Mind

The mind plays an extremely important part in our emotions. The mind determines how we are going to respond emotionally to situations. What we think steers us into how we feel. "It is the cognition which determines whether the state of physiological arousal will be labeled as 'anger' 'joy' 'fear' or whatever," according to Stanley Schacter and Jerome Singer in *Behavior Change Through Self Control.* The anxiety of riding a roller coaster may be labeled as joy to one person and desperate panic to another.

Irrational ideas cause a tremendous amount of internal suffering during divorce. The following chapter will list specific irrational ideas which set up stumbling blocks. Irrational ideas, black-and-white thinking, over-generalizations, and excessive reliance on others' judgments form demons in our minds. All four of these mind monsters need to be purged in divorce so that you can progress.

Irrational Ideas

Self-verbalizations may greatly enhance or soundly defeat an individual. One can appreciably control one's own feelings by controlling one's thoughts. Each individual has his or her own set of cognitions that helps to interpret data coming in through the senses.

A person who feels that divorce, for example, means failing at marriage will feel guilty about the divorce. "I feel that I should have been able to resolve our conflicts," the self-deprecating statement would go. A second person may consider that divorce is a natural outgrowth of persons changing within a marriage and thus classify divorce as a rational, mature, problem-solving alternative. How do these two differ internally by just having that one different thought about the same event?

The first person (with guilt) would be likely to define things as terrible while the second (without guilt) would define them as inconvenient. The first person would hedge and feel uncomfortable when admitting his or her divorce to an admired stranger. The second would readily and acceptingly acknowledge the divorce. The first person would also use the data to devalue himself or herself in not living up to the ideal; the second person would blend the information nonjudgmentally into his or her self-concept.

The irrational thinking differs radically from rational thinking. Rational thinking is tranquil, usually problem-solving in nature, less personalized and elicits few emotions. Emotional or irrational thinking is a kind of appraisal thinking. Value judgments are always implied. The thinking is highly personalized and is used to determine self-worth. Each emotionally loaded thought usually is a hand-me-down from parents, church or community. Examples are, "Long-haired boys are weird," "A grade of C is terrible," "Something is wrong with people who are divorced."

Example: Clyde. He feels deprived because his wife does not cook for him. He regularly tells himself, "If my wife loved me and valued me, she would cook more for me." The underlying irrational thought is that in order to feel loved, Clyde has to be waited on.

Diane circulates another irrational thought in her marriage: "I must not have enough appeal to attract my husband anymore; he stays at the office just to avoid me. A husband should put his family first." The irrational thoughts with which Diane is driving herself crazy are: First, "My husband should not want to avoid me." Second, "He should put his family above work." Her husband may not have bought the same set of "shoulds" as a child. Most emotional thoughts can be traced back to shoulds.

Albert Ellis, a noted psychologist, has devised a whole therapy treatment program, Rational-Emotive Therapy, which is based on this irrational thinking. He maintains that controlling illogical thoughts frees the person of self-defeating thinking and behavior. Ellis in his book *Reason and Emotion in Psychotherapy* states that ". . . if certain negative emotions are highly unpleasant states which add little to human happiness and make the world a poorer place in which to live, wise people should presumably make a conscious effort to change their internalized senses with which they often create their negative emotions."

In Rational-Emotive Therapy, you change your emotionally-laden, self-defeating internal messages to yourself and you are cured. In terms of dealing with depression, guilt and anger, Ellis's system has merit. If you will search through your own experience you will find that the prelude to a depression, to guilt or to anger is invariably accompanied by at least one self-defeating, highly personalized thought that is repeated over and over again. These thoughts usually stoke the fires of emotions.

Ellis lists some irrational thoughts which are common and which are also used by an individual to drive himself or herself crazy. In both the period during which a person is deciding on whether to separate or not and also the postseparation period, these thoughts may run rampant. While such thoughts are common in all of us, the vulnerability experienced in a period of divorce fosters their repetition. The key to climbing out of postmarital self-torture is to flip the record over and play the more constructive side. Let us take a look at some of the more typical irrational ideas:

(1) "I have to be loved in order to survive." The contrast is concentrating on self-love, self-respect, giving and loving.

Barry, a client, illustrates the repetition of this irrational thought. "She doesn't love me any more. Two years ago she would have remembered my birthday. I can't stand the thought of her falling out of love with me. If she is no longer in love with me, I'll fall apart. I'll put pressure on her to love me so I can get that feeling back from her. How could she? After all I've done for her? I can't imagine how she could just fall out of love. Without that, I don't have anything."

Barry longingly and angrily searches for more examples to support the thesis of Marie not loving him any more. Little insignificant incidents now become significant. He develops his case of being unloved much like a lawyer would dig up the facts. Any kind word or deed does not register so as not to contaminate the evidence.

Eventually Marie is made aware of the process, first because of Barry's sulking and then through a verbal assault of the evidence. The abuse becomes severe and prolonged. Marie starts losing respect for the hurting Barry. During this process, damage is done to Barry, Marie and their relationship. The damage done to Barry stems from the inordinate time and energy he spends concentrating on what he thinks Marie is doing to him. Little time is spent on his own self-improvement, doing things that would help him gain self-respect and respect from other sources than Marie.

Barry pulls back from his friends in order to more carefully scrutinize Marie. He is so consumed in watching her that he loses interest in his hobbies, his work or cultivating new friendships. He is concentrating so hard on being loved that he has a hard time loving. The absent loving behaviors on his part make him more susceptible to not being loved. His self-esteem further diminishes. With reduced self-esteem, he feels even more desperate about restoring his losses.

This process can be reversed if Barry would step out of his lawyer garb and try to do those things that he accuses his wife of not doing. Paying attention to work, hobbies, children and other friends in an effort to better oneself generates self-respect. Temporarily, Barry needed to give up the idea of *having* to be loved.

What happened in reality in Barry's case was that Marie was temporarily preoccupied by her work. She felt extremely pressured and overwrought by what was happening on the job. With hardly enough energy to survive work, Marie felt that she needed time out from showing love to Barry. Underneath the preoccupation, the love lay dormant, waiting until the work pressures eased. Barry was finally convinced that he had to give up the thought that he had to be loved. He let Marie work through the turmoil she was in at work and was even able to help her resolve the conflict sooner. Helping her added to Barry's feelings of self-worth. Barry indeed did not *have* to be loved in order to survive. Love for mature adults is not a dire necessity like food, water and sleep.

(2) "He or she was brutally wrong, villainous and wicked. He or she should be severely punished for what

was done to me in the marriage." The contrary way of assessing another's behavior is that certain acts are inappropriate or antisocial, and the people who perform such acts are uninformed or emotionally disturbed.

Pete, an electrician, was engaged in a casual affair which turned into genuine love. Joanne, his wife, discovered the affair and branded him a villain who deserved to be hanged. She considered him vile and wicked. That was it! The marriage was over. She wasn't going to live with that evil person.

Pete may indeed have violated the marital commitment by secretly having an affair and falling in love with another woman. Joanne had two choices, though, when she found out about the affair. First, she could destroy the relationship by blaming Pete for what he had done and by not forgiving him. (She chose this alternative.) Since Pete was more likely than not to feel guilty anyway, this choice made it harder for him to remain in contact with Joanne, since she was a constant reminder of that guilt. In this case, Pete was not only getting blamed for having the affair, but his total character was being vilified with harsh accusations.

Joanne did have a second choice. She could make Pete aware of her feelings and the ultimate consequences of his behavior without painting him totally black. If the affair was casual and nonmeaningful to Pete, it would have given him a chance to rectify his behavior and save the marital relationship. Often a stronger relationship results by working through painful problems.

Cast as the villain, though, Pete had few opportunities to convince Joanne of his heartfelt desire to stay married to her. Since Joanne had made public the injustice done her, Pete felt alienated not only from her but from friends. He had little choice but to leave the marriage and seek refuge with his paramour. The switch was almost mandatory in order to escape the constant bombardment of slanderous remarks.

Joanne could have saved the marriage, herself and Pete if she had viewed the hurtful situation as just that. Having an affair didn't make Pete a complete villain. Joanne was blaming Pete because of her sense of being betrayed and because of her fear of loss. Renegotiating the marital contract so that affairs were permissible for both parties might have been one way to correct the injustice. As it was, Joanne suffered what she feared most—losing Pete—because she could not get out of her mind the thought that she had been wronged. If Joanne started from the assumption that Pete was uninformed, emotionally distraught or acting inappropriately, she would have been half-way home in helping Pete work it through. She would then become an active participant in the conflict rather than feeling abused.

(3) "If things do not go (or stay) the way I very much want them to, it would be horrible and catastrophic." The opposite of that irrational belief is that, yes, it is inconvenient when things are not the way one would like them to be. One should certainly try to change or control conditions so that they become more satisfactory. But, if changing or controlling uncomfortable situations is impossible, one had better become resigned to their existence and stop telling oneself how awful they are.

One example of this irrational thinking was found in two clients involved in counseling. Ted was constantly telling himself how awful it was that Sue had to spend almost all of her time as an intern at the hospital. She was on call for a week at a time and lived in the hospital dormitories provided for interns. Ted was hurt, frustrated, angry and resentful that he was spending so much of his time and energy waiting for her. During these long hours, he would keep repeating to himself how terrible his situation was. Even though he knew that the internship would be over in a year and that the schedule would be more relaxed, he constantly threw temper tantrums because he was not able to get his way. The alternative for Ted was to resign himself to these less-than-desirable conditions and stop telling himself how horrible they were. He was indeed driving himself crazy with these thoughts.

A second example of this hanging on to a self-destructive idea was a forty-year-old woman who had a hard time letting go of the idea that being a divorced mother was a horrible fate. She had enjoyed being married; her self-concept centered very much around providing a nice home for her husband and children. She enjoyed entertaining her husband's business guests.

The state of being single was intolerable. Instead of accepting this condition (being single) which she could not immediately change, she was so obsessed with her singleness that it became impossible to relate to other people. She was so full of anger at the thought of being single that she was not receptive to others. She had first to give up the thought that it was intolerable to be without a whole family before she could get out of herself enough to even notice other men. She finally let go of the fight and accepted the fact that she could put up with a less than ideal situation for her. "Yes, I'm single and that is not my preferable mode. But I can accept being single as a less-than-desirable condition for me and not continue fighting it." Two months passed. She then met a man whom she later married.

Much of this trouble is seen in clients who have been overindulged in childhood and have not learned to settle for a life that is less than ideal. Divorce forces them to learn to.

(4) "Human unhappiness is externally caused and I

cannot control it." The converse of that point of view is "virtually all human unhappiness is caused or sustained by the view one takes of things rather than the things themselves."

The bittersweet taste of a former marriage can be caused by this idea that human unhappiness is caused by something the spouse does or does not do. One comment I have heard from divorcing clients is, "For the last few years, I have been made miserable. I have lost the best part of my life because of living with him or her." Inherent in this statement is putting all of the responsibility for happiness on the spouse. The victim is freed of the role in playing the victim.

While this tendency to project responsibility for wrongdoing is common, it is not particularly healthy. In order to be ruthless, one needs a volunteer victim. The roles are complementary, one cannot exist without the other. Calling oneself the victim is a passive way of not taking responsibility for what has happened.

You may not know how to be a nonvictim. In Chapter 5, "Behavior Control," self-assertion is described, if this is your problem. More often, though, the victim role has a payoff. One female client quite openly admitted that the security and comfort of knowing how to respond in that role was much more important to her than giving it up. At least she did not torture herself with the thought that her position was superimposed by her husband; she deliberately chose the victim role.

American culture is finally growing away from the thought that you can best live by serving someone else and making that person(s) happy. We are coming back to the thought that each person is responsible for his or her own happiness. Only then can two persons come together in strength and give self-made happiness to each other. William Masters and Virginia Johnson, the noted sex researchers, documented this in a recent presentation in Atlanta, Georgia.) They both commented that, in sex, prevailing attitudes had changed from: two generations ago you did sex "to" a partner; one generation ago you did sex "for" a partner; and now the trend is to do it "with" a partner. Marriage gradually is changing along those same lines; each person is responsible for creating his or her own happiness.

(5) "One should remain upset if faced with a dangerous or fearsome reality." The healthy counterpart is that if something is dangerous or fearsome, one should frankly face it and render it nondangerous.

A person in a dead marriage frequently suffers this. Instead of taking a deep breath, buoying up courage and breaking out of the marriage, the person unhappily dreams about it, and worries about the dangers. The anticipation of being alone is dreadful.

I have found that most often the anticipation is far more devastating than the reality. The more a person anticipates separation with morbid fears, the more panicky he or she becomes. Fear of loneliness is much greater than the loneliness itself. Fear of not meeting financial obligations is much more of an obstacle than running behind on bills. Fear of what the parents will say when they find out that you have separated is much greater than the real parental repercussions. The huge nightmarish image of separation turns into a period of time where you manage the little problems as they arise. Fairly often a feeling of confidence and relief will ensue after the person has been handling these real problems.

One female client, after getting a divorce, went through a rugged anticipation of having to work for the first time in fifteen years. She feared she would not be able to do a good job, that her skills were rusty, and that would displease her boss. Finally she worried about not being able to commit herself to a 40-hour work week. Two weeks after her first job began, she was pleased, relaxed, highly acclaimed and managing just beautifully.

(6) "Human happiness can be achieved by sitting and waiting for it." The converse is humans tend to be happiest when they are actively and vitally absorbed in creative pursuits, or when they are devoting themselves to people or projects outside themselves.

One of the worst things a divorcing person can do is to cut himself or herself off from a job, interests, friends, hobbies and/or children, and totally turn inward. Learning from the experience and dealing with emotions are a part of divorce. But, not to the exclusion of all else. I have had a couple of clients who were convinced when they first arrived in my office that total isolation and contemplation about the previous marriage were going to be helpful. For a short time, they were. An exclusive diet of insight over a long period of time makes it quite difficult to shed. The inactivity, excessive time to think, lack of feedback from other persons, lack of confidence gained by successful outside ventures, all contribute to a demonic imagination that can unrealistically twist the facts.

William Goode reported in his study of divorced women that those women who got into activities following the divorce that allowed them to meet new people had the easiest time adjusting to divorce. In my experience, I have also found that those persons who over-schedule themselves with activity adjust much better to being alone. With other persons, one can try out new behaviors, learn to adapt to new people, and accumulate experience with change. Completely alone, one has no testing grounds. While time out to think, restore and grow normally lasts a couple of months in the postmarital period, an excess of this can bring a downward spiral of emotion that becomes increasingly difficult to reverse.

(7) "I have no control over my emotions. I cannot help feeling certain things." The opposite thought, of course, is that one has enormous control over one's own emotions but only if one so chooses. Learning when to start the reversal process and practicing are the elements of control.

While it is harmless to allow oneself to be saddened by a divorce, or grieved by the loss of someone, or elated over the relief provided by divorce, or depressed by loneliness, many people cannot differentiate between accepting that mood and controlling it. "If I let myself get depressed, then I will be devastated. I will not be able to maintain my job and will have to quit the world for awhile." These words reflect someone who is afraid of depression and tries to run away from it because he or she feels a lack in being able to control it.

Accepting a negative emotion means giving it its just due. Accepting depression, for instance, means being able to appreciate the need for it at the time, get into it and let it exhaust itself. You feel no shame about being depressed; no guilt, no anger, no fear, no embarrassment. Just pure unadulterated sadness. These secondary feelings (anger, guilt, fear) about a primary mood, depression in this case, cause much more difficulty than the mood itself.

Controlling the feeling involves deciding that you have learned enough from it and it is time to step in and change it. Practicing healthier self-statements is one way of reversing the deepening blackness.

I have watched many clients in divorce try to fight their emotions. One client, Sally, was afraid of becoming depressed and lost, so she waged full-scale war against the feeling. Eventually, it sneaked up behind her when she wasn't expecting it and insisted on being felt. Fighting the mood only compounds the energy required to deal with it.

You do indeed have control over your feelings. You may not be experienced at controlling them, or accepting them for that matter. These skills can be self-taught.

(8) "I have a true, consistent self which, if I could just find it, would cure me of all this floundering." No. Each person does not have a strictly consistent internal self which one always behaves in accordance with. Individuals are complex composites of all the emotions and the true process of living is accepting and experiencing one's emotional and intellectual shifts.

This irrational idea is why it is so difficult for many people to see how divorce can be both excruciatingly painful and personally creative; both grief-filled and a relief, both a period of being vulnerable and confidence-building. Divorce is a composite of feelings, perhaps intensified but hardly ever perfectly consistent.

Many persons during divorce tend to want to simplify their recollection of the marital experience. Mary values it as "a dreadful experience." She comments, "I couldn't believe that I stuck it out in such a losing relationship." Mary's need to evaluate the marriage as entirely horrible was her attempt to become consistent.

While other persons are more complex in their evaluations of the marriage, the person who over-simplifies it by saying how hateful it was is usually trying to mask an unresolved attraction to the ex-spouse. The couple would not have married or gotten together if some sort of positive bond did not exist. As a person distances the hurts of divorce, the perceptions become more clear. The spouse is then seen more objectively, with both the desirable and undesirable qualities.

Burt, for instance, went into a hate vendetta when he was divorced from Laura. He accused her of spending money recklessly, taking advantage of him when he gave her free financial authority and hosts of other ills. The resentment was so powerful by the time of their divorce that he could hardly remember any virtues in her. Once the anger cooled, he was able to see why he had been attracted to her in the first place. Her charm. Her wit. Her graciousness as a hostess. Distance allowed Burt to hold both good and bad memories of Laura in his mind at the same time. Actually Burt had also been attracted to Laura's careless attitude about money and originally was attracted to her because of her lack of frugal habits. Burt finally recognized that the financial recklessness of Laura had indeed attracted him. Accepting that one behavior or desire can be both attractive and unattractive at the same time is an example of accepting internal inconsistency. Divorce has enough of them.

Thoughts and feelings about a love triangle represent another example of difficulties with others' inconsistencies. Beverly, for instance, had been having an affair with Dick. Her husband, Mike, thought that it was humanly impossible for Beverly to love both himself and Dick. If we carefully examine the word "love" we can· see how emotionally unrefined our language is. Beverly was perfectly capable of loving both Mike and Dick at the same time. The love might simply be different for each man. In this case, the love Beverly felt for Mike, her husband, was a deeper, more secure, and meaningful love while the love for Dick was intense, sexual and more of an infatuation.

Mike couldn't understand this inconsistency. "How could she love both of us at the same time?" Mike was unable to differentiate the love Beverly had for him as opposed to the love she had for Dick. The irrational thought "She couldn't love both of us" eventually drove him into an unnecessary divorce.

(9) "The world is always fair. Justice and mercy will triumph." There is absolutely no evidence to support this conclusion. Likewise, the definition of "fair" is different for different people.

If you are hooked on complete justice during divorce you are headed for big trouble. Inequities may be unresolved in a divorce settlement. A wife putting her husband through graduate school feels like she has sacrificed time and energy to enable him to complete school. At the end of school, he decides that she does not live up to his intellectual standards and leaves. She feels unjustly treated and victimized. She cannot believe that there has been no compensation for her. Frequently, though, fairness does not triumph and justice does not prevail.

Fighting an irresoluble injustice can be like kicking a stone statue. The only thing that gets hurt is the one who is doing the kicking. Having the wisdom to let go when a person or circumstance is unchangeable is an important element of mental health.

In trying to correct the injustices of divorce, there is a mountain of examples. The husband tries to weasel his way out of child support even though he loves his children. The wife lies about how much money she has secretly saved. The husband screams about his wife's failings to friends and neighbors. The wife harasses the husband by cancelling out his visitation rights at the last minute.

The end result of trying to mend the injustice is that the person trying it feels horrible about himself or herself. "I know I shouldn't treat him or her like this. I really feel awful about what I have become."

The trick when you feel maligned is to let go. So

this time you were the one with the short end of the stick. So what? Next time just work a little harder at maintaining a balance all the way through.

Black-and-White Thinking

Black-and-white thinking happens when a person or event is considered all right or all wrong.

With our Puritan habit of placing emphasis on right and wrong, good and evil, we engage in making many value judgments. Unfortunately, a few people have trouble breaking their judgments down into more than two categories. Previous examples used in this book are good indicators: "Our marriage was not totally good so it must have been totally bad." "She had an affair with another man and therefore didn't love me." "He gave money and time to charities so therefore he was a totally virtuous person." Another dichotomous reasoning trick is to say, "He forgot to pick up the laundry so he doesn't love me enough to remember." The thought pattern in this self-talk is that the other is either totally loving and preoccupied with me or the other doesn't love me at all.

In dichotomous thinking, the words "always" and "never" are common. "He always put me down." "She never appreciated anything I did for her."

Learning to differentiate the degrees in a situation is an important step in reducing the tension that causes these dichotomous thoughts. "She was appreciative 30 percent of the time and I needed more than that." "He put me down on social occasions just because *he* was feeling inferior." "Divorce can be a mature way of problem-solving for some and a cop-out for others." These statements allow for more openness, tolerance, and fewer anxiety-accompanied thoughts. Black-and-white thinking sends you racing into either-or emotional judgments.

Overgeneralization

Making overgeneralizations and dichotomous think-ing are somewhat related in that they both involve exag-geration. Dichotomous reasoning views individuals as either good or bad, while an overgeneralization says "All of the same category are the same way"; "All persons who are divorced have immature personalities"; "All mothers love their children"; "All insurance salesmen are crooked."

The problem with making overgeneralizations lies in the process of the dissolution that results from the hurts that are residual. If one spouse has been hurt and mistreated by the other, a common generalization is for that spouse to say, "I just don't trust men or women anymore." I have seen many clients take a long time to get rid of their negative emotions and to see clearly that some persons are to be trusted and others are not but to one *degree* or another. Another troublesome over-generalization comes from the anticipation of being single again. Such overgeneralizations as, "Poor people are unhappy," make the individual fear the financial strain that divorce is going to impose. One guilt-producing overgeneralization comes from the old myth that fatherless boys or motherless girls end up emotion-ally disturbed. While children are affected by the absence of one parent, the effects are complex and dependent on many factors (the emotional stability of the remaining parent, the acceptance of that parent of the opposite sex, the exposure of the child to healthy models of the opposite sex, the peer relations of the child and so forth).

Making overgeneralizations poses another problem for a person who is divorcing or divorced. Other per-sons, including friends, relatives, strangers, coworkers and children, also make overgeneralizations about di-vorced persons. These stereotypes about divorced people vary from "They must be miserable" to "They must be living it up with a wild set of singles, loving every minute of freedom" to "They are irresponsible because they are divorced" to "They are part of the modern set of divorced people." Divorcing or divorced people are faced with modifying friends', parents', and coworkers' stereotypes so they will not be prejudged or misinterpreted. How very many times I have heard a divorcing person say, "I feel that I am making the best decision possible for me. But I do feel guilty about not feeling guilty."

Other significant persons expected that individual to feel guilty and ashamed. How do you tell people that you are not feeling the way their stereotype says you are supposed to feel? That specific method will be further amplified in the next chapter. Making your feelings and wishes known without putting the other person down is the key. To allow yourself to be stereotyped without trying to change other people's stereotypes is a lonely experience. Divorced persons often report feeling misunderstood and separated from their close friends because of the absence of a learned communication mechanism for corrective feedback.

Excessive Reliance on Others

"Overconcern about public opinion is one of the most widespread maladies." The whole second section of this book demonstrates the paramount importance of values that society and parents inculcate in their children and how these are likely to affect feelings about a subject like divorce. If those instructions are further accompanied by such statements as, "What will the neighbors think?" "Your grandfather would be so ashamed of you," "How can you make me look bad in front of all those other parents?" then the recipient is likely to develop a bad case of excessive reliance on others' judgments as he or she grows older. While the decision and process of divorce may feel perfectly comfortable for that individual, the concern about others' opinions produces great trauma. Trying to please yourself, your children, your friends, relatives and spouse becomes impossible because behaving in any one way is likely to displease at least one other person in this group. One behavior sequence I have noticed in therapy concerns those who try too hard to please other people. They end up doing nothing, making no decisions, offending no one, but becoming miserable in the process. They are immobilized by the impossibility that one person could jump on four different horses and ride in four different directions simultaneously. Rather than choose one horse, they deliberate. This kind of paralyzed thinking is too painful for most people to keep up for long.

Internalizing a set of personalized values that represents a strong inner core allows a person to have confidence and a feeling of inner security. In order to have this strong inner core, a person needs to develop an ability to make decisions for oneself, to have opinions, to have some predictable ways of behaving. Being a solid person means that a few people are going to be alienated and some are going to dislike you. For most people, that experience is painful at first but not anywhere near as devastating as the anxiety concomitant with trying constantly to please others.

Dealing with the difficult decision about which spouse is going to get the children is a good example of how these dynamics operate. One female client did not want her children, felt that her husband was a much better parent than she and knew that he wanted the children. Yet she would not give them up because she was so afraid of what others would think of her. The end result was her taking out her resentment on her children as she unwillingly mothered them. Another male client wanted one child and wanted the mother to have the other, which was equitable with her. Both parents feared, though, what others would say about splitting the children up, so both partners ended up more dissatisfied while the children went with the mother.

Chapter 5
Behavior Control

Change your behavior, and your emotions and attitudes normally shift in that direction. Tom, for instance, set a goal for himself to become a more giving person. Buying birthday and Christmas gifts for his wife, his parents and relatives elicited strong anxiety in Tom because he was deathly afraid of not buying an appropriate gift.

Rather than going ahead and taking the risk, Tom learned how to worry excessively, then berate himself around the time that he was supposed to be out shopping. The result was that Tom consistently turned up for celebrations empty-handed.

Tom set goals for himself to buy more gifts. Nonholidays were less risky so he decided to start with nonbirthday presents. Gradually he built up to buying the desired Christmas and birthday presents. As Tom increased his gift-buying behavior, he gained confidence in his ability to overcome his self-imposed obstacle; he gained approval from those receiving the gifts; and he gradually relaxed about what was once an onerous task.

Increasing his gift-buying behavior helped to

change Tom's feelings and attitudes. While that doesn't work in 100 percent of the cases, increasing the desired behavior usually does affect feelings and attitudes.

The more dimensions (attitude, feelings, and behavior) that you can work on at once, the easier it is to change. For instance, if Tom had practiced relaxing himself as he thought about what gift to buy, the behavioral change would have come even faster. Coupling that with the third dimension—self-verbalizations—makes the change even faster. Tom learned to give up the sentence he constantly said to himself when thinking about what to buy. "I know he or she won't like it." He might replace that failure statement with something like "I know he or she will appreciate my affection that I show through this gift."

Personality change can be fun and also a challenge. The simple behaviors, thoughts, and emotions appear as stars seen through a telescope. Simple behaviors from a long distance look small and innocuous, Close up, they can be powerful, destructive, fiery masses.

How do you change these little habits so that you can work towards your goal of becoming a more effective you? This chapter will address itself to how you can apply behavioral-control techniques to personality change.

Reminder: The goal is to learn how to analyze your pain in order to discover the goals which are basic to you. Then learn how to change your self-verbalizations and behaviors in the direction that will guarantee reaching those goals.

Setting Goals

Great pleasure is derived from anticipation. Anticipation plays an important role in the reward of a habit. We look forward to the gratification, whether that gratification stems from reducing a primary drive (like hunger, thirst or sex), or satisfying a curiosity drive. Unlike less intelligent animals, we can stretch the pleasureful part of a habit over time. Before the event occurs, we pleasurefully anticipate. Afterwards the warmth of the event is relived in memory.

Setting goals is a means of pleasureful anticipation. It also takes you out of thinking about the past and thrusts you into thinking more happily towards the future.

Three steps are necessary in order to set goals. The first is to determine the desired outcome. For instance, a divorced person might decide to increase self-esteem. The second step is to specify what behaviors are necessary in order to achieve that goal. Increased self-esteem for one person might mean (1) an increase in the number of positive thoughts; (2) a decrease in physiological tension when talking to new acquaintances; (3) a greater frequency of initiating conversations and activities.

Once the general goal is broken down into particularly desirable behaviors, the third step is to delineate what specific behaviors are going to help achieve that goal. The first goal might be achieved by actively working on decreasing negative self-evaluations repeated internally, and immediately supplanting the negative thought with a positive one. "I'm a dull person," for instance, might be kicked out and replaced by "I do indeed have something to give." You might then go out and read up on current events or remember an interesting story which backed up your thought. Or learn to lend your ear to another.

Another handle in getting rid of failure thoughts might be to seek a new vocational direction. Feeling a solid vocational identity helps to overcome emptiness and subsequent loss of self-esteem. Decreased tension follows from feeling worthwhile at the job.

Phase three of building self-esteem, in this particular instance, might be learning self-assertion. Learning how to say no. Learning how to ask for what you want. The last part of this chapter more specifically outlines a program for enhanced self-assertion.

While setting goals sounds simple, defining behaviors in specific terms is not. The more specifically the behaviors are stated, the easier the goal is to tackle. You can likewise measure your success readily by how many of these little units you have accomplished. It requires careful analysis of complicated objectives. If you find that you are having trouble setting small, obtainable goals that are easy to work with, a therapist can come in handy. Therapists are usually skilled at helping you break down impossible or overwhelming goals into manageable units.

What Goals? Self-Inventory

What kinds of goals should you set? The place to look for the kinds of change you want is in those areas which have caused you pain. One client, for instance, made constant demands on her husband to be open with her. She was an expressive, warm individual who shared her every feeling with her husband. Her own barometer of success was how much she enticed her husband to reveal himself to her on an emotional level. Every time he would begin to open up, though, she would escalate her demands to the point that it sounded like criticism to him. He drew his emotional cloak around himself tighter and tighter. He found a woman who did not make the kind of demands his wife did and allowed him to volunteer his feelings.

In the pain of being cut off, Margaret learned that she needed to know when and how to pull back. She needed to develop the sensitivity to know when her desire became a suffocating demand. Margaret got in touch with that necessary sense of timing in the depths of postmarital depression. From then on, she set a goal for herself that she wanted to become more controlled and sensitive to others. When she felt her tenaciousness welling up inside, she learned how to stop it, turn around and withdraw from pressuring. That left her new mate free to come to her and volunteer his feelings.

Goals may be anything from becoming more or less domineering, indecisive, passive, idealistic, expressive, tolerant, carefree, alert, conversational, trusting, self-confident, cheerful, stable, conforming, mature, tense, fearful, casual, motivated, structured, any personality characteristic which would enhance your own effectiveness. Each one of these goals can be broken down into specific desirable behaviors which help you achieve your stated goal.

If you find you are having trouble reaching your goals, you may have one of two problems. Your goals may not be your own—they were set by forces outside of you like parents or society. Or, your goals were too big.

Divorce is a perfect time for setting new goals. I have witnessed a tremendous amount of personality growth during this period because people set new goals for themselves. The old system that reinforced bad habits is no longer interfering with growth. New friends can be chosen to model and reinforce those characteristics which you desire in yourself. One's lifestyle is usually disrupted enough by divorce that the old habits are shaken up and can be resettled into new, more effective patterns. Other friends anticipate a little change so they allow for new feelings, behaviors and attitudes to emerge without expecting all of the old ones.

Breaking Habits

Most people do not realize what pleasure their simple habits give them until they try to change one. Smoking is an extreme example. I would imagine that you can sit back and enumerate dozens of habits that are part of your everyday life—from whom you eat lunch with, what kinds of foods you eat, your morning getting-ready-for-the-day ritual, what path you take to work, how you organize your day, how and when you open your mail, how you pace yourself during the day and so forth. When people divorce, their habits are abruptly changed. Separation may mean a different car pool with new drivers, new friends, different eating schedules, the loss of some habits centering around affection and sex. Instead you have to find new ways of finding attention, new habits of meeting and getting to know people and adjusting to new schedules.

Learning how to change habits with more ease and facility becomes important when so many of them need changing.

Habits have payoffs or rewards. No matter how destructive or painful the habit appears to be on the surface, you can be sure there is some kind of pleasure derived from it. One female client could not understand why she kept on screaming at her little girl upon the slightest provocation. The screaming was nonproductive and usually elicited the same in her daughter. Everytime, though, when the child started making demands on the mother to give her attention the mother would throw a temper tantrum.

The mother was a highly educated, intelligent, well-controlled person in every other setting but this. She felt guilty about being an excellent teacher and not being able to control her temper with her own child. The habit of screaming had acquired some strength over time. By the time I saw the mother the habit was well-entrenched. While the habit appeared totally useless on the surface to this woman, the behaviors were tension-reducing for her. She felt purged of anger. Anger that had been saved up all day from one little irritation to another. The angry explosion rid her of this stored-up anger.

In order to break the habit, she needed to find a substitute for the pleasure-producing side of the habit. Releasing these stored bits of anger in little pieces as the anger arose proved to be the solution.

The essential element in changing habits is to substitute another habit in its place which is equally desirable. Try to rate the now inappropriate habit on a scale of one to ten in terms of the pleasure you derived from it. Then think up a new sequence of behaviors that produces the same degree of pleasure and plan that as a replacement.

One divorced client used to come home from work at 6 p.m. and lie down with her husband. They would relax on the bed and talk about the day's happenings. The payoff was unwinding in a relaxed and meaningful way.

When they divorced, she continued to crawl onto the bed when she got home. Instead of its being pleasureful, she found that she became obsessed about the marriage. These thoughts would catapult her into depression. Yet the continuation of the habit still had enough payoff to make her automatically head for the bed when she arrived home.

Changing that no longer appropriate habit involved assessing what else would help her relax in the same way. She rated her pleasureful relaxing activities on a scale of one to ten and discovered that stopping by the community swimming pool before she went home would serve a similar purpose. Replacing the old inappropriate habit then became pleasureful.

Richard, another client, had a habit after his divorce of calling his ex-wife whenever he started feeling lonely. She had made it clear that she wanted no part in working through his depressed feelings but he continued to call her. The telephone calls were painful to Richard. He often was further rebuffed and let down. After the call, he would inevitably feel worse.

Movies were pleasureful for Richard. He did not mind going alone. His habit-breaking consisted of replacing the telephoning with a movie. Whenever he felt the surge of loneliness rise that prompted him to telephone Patti, he would instead take off for the movies. Gradually the periods of loneliness spaced themselves farther and farther apart. From this, he salvaged his relationship with Patti by not making unreasonable requests.

Stimulus Control

Stimulus control is helpful in removing the oppressive nature of divorce. Stimulus control is controlling your environment so as few painful cues as possible surround you.

If the separation has left you surrounded by reminders which throw you into depression or anger, you are a prime candidate for stimulus control. The underlying theory here is that in order to curtail behavior we must detach it from its controlling stimuli. Eating at the dinner table at night, for instance, may have been an extremely pleasureful stimulus. Now you are alone. That same dinner table reminds you of what you have lost. Approaching dinnertime and that dinner table alone spirals you downward into a depression.

Phil, for example, enjoyed tremendously taking a hot bath with his wife. They would relax, talk and play while bathing. When Phil's wife left, Phil and the bathtub remained. Every time he approached that bathtub after separation, tears would well up in his eyes. It was all he could do to climb in the tub.

Life is full of reminders after separation. A type of car. A holiday. A song. A flower. Dinnertime. A special kind of laugh. The bed. A mannerism that you loved. A building. A time of year. A sport. With heightened emotionality immediately following separation, these memory traces of your former spouse can be hard to take. All these carry some stimulus which triggers pleasant or unpleasant memories. The pleasant ones are harder to handle because they remind you of the loss.

Changing the cues provides a way to avoid triggering the memories constantly.

Whoever leaves the house, if any feelings are left over after the divorce, has the distinct advantage. Departing spouses can surround themselves with cues which are not loaded. They can decorate the new house or apartment with new self-expressive furnishings.

Often the best thing a person can do after a separation is to change living quarters. While our old Puritan ethic may call this running away, it really does facilitate the adjustment period. The old cues and reminders are left behind so the past doesn't constantly haunt. After the emotionality has died and a detachment has set in, the old cues lose their value.

For some persons, this isn't a problem. For others the apartment or house can be like a tomb. He or she dreads coming home after work. If there is little choice because of financial constraints in finding a new environment, you can also mitigate this pain by learning the relaxation technique. Reread Chapter 3 and apply it to the cues which produce anxiety at home.

Role Rehearsal

(Role rehearsal is a way of practicing the behavior changes in a safe place before you try the big time.)

Many clients I have seen report that the period of postdivorce is like a second adolescence. "I feel like a teen-ager all over again," many have said with amusement and surprise. These clients ranged in age from twenty to fifty-five. With the excitement and challenge came a feeling of vulnerability. "Oh, oh. I can get hurt again. I don't have a spouse to go home to who will help me lick my wounds."

The feeling of vulnerability revolves, to a great extent, around dating. Wondering whether the person you met will telephone. Uncertainty about whether the person is attracted enough physically to cross that line. Being afraid of rejection. The period of divorce carries a great deal of ambiguity with it.

The old behaviors produced fairly predictable responses. You knew what turned your spouse on and off. Now you have to start all over again with new people. The same responses you gave which turned your ex-spouse on may turn this date off.

Ferreting out what pleases and displeases new acquaintances feels much like role rehearsal. You try on certain behaviors to see whether or not they get rewarded. If they do, you repeat them. But the finding out elicits feelings of "Maybe that will turn him or her off." Uncertainty is a big part of it.

And so it is with behaviors that you seek purposely to change for the better. You choose one goal and the behaviors which will help you get to that goal. Now you have to try out those behaviors on people when it not only feels strange but when you have no idea how that new behavior will come across.

Take Marcia, for instance. She was a very shy person who felt intimidated by her in-laws. She anticipated every visit with tension and resentment at their condescending attitudes towards her. She wanted an equal relationship with them but constantly found herself inhibiting her opinions and avoiding confrontations.

Divorce left her husband with the children. She had visiting rights but found herself exposed to the anger-arousing in-laws whenever she visited. While she was deathly afraid that changing her behavior would release her rage, she did want to be able to express herself without feeling so stifled.

Role rehearsal with a friend of hers allowed Marcia to practice asserting some of her own opinions in a safe place. Her friend gave her feedback as to when the openness sounded aggressive and attacking. Safe rehearsal and Marcia was on her way to trying it with the in-laws.

At first, the in-laws were surprised at the sudden change but they learned to respect Marcia for having her own opinions. The confrontations were not hostile and destructive but engendered closeness.

Role rehearsal feels strange, awkward and unnatural at first. Clients sometimes retort with a statement like "This isn't *me*. I can't be something other than me." Yes, you can! The new behavior does indeed feel new like a combination of the adolescent vulnerability and being an actor or actress. With practice, the new behaviors come more easily and feel more natural. Whenever you have these two feelings of adolescence and vulnerability, you know that you are ripe for change. Repetition and receiving rewards from the outside jell the behaviors into your new, more effective personality.

Assertive Training

One quality that I have consistently found problematic in persons suffering in a prolonged manner after a divorce is their ability to assert themselves. Much of the anger at the ex-spouse can be attributed to a passivity which allowed the ex-spouse to control the relationship disproportionately. The end result is resentment against self and the ex-spouse for having been manipulated. Often needs were neither clearly expressed nor met.

The ability to stand up and ask for what is rightfully yours without being aggressive about it is the last phase of self-improvement for the divorcing person. Dr. Jan Kelley, a counseling psychologist at Georgia State University, has developed an assertive-training program which plots out a course in assertiveness. The modified version presented here will aid in self-respect, respect from others, a feeling of confidence and a sense of mastery. All of these combined add up to a stronger, more confident, identity.

Definition: First, it is important to differentiate nonassertiveness and assertiveness from aggression. Many people are frightened about being assertive because they feel it will look or sound like an attack. So, instead of expressing true feelings, they suppress them in nonassertive behavior. In assertiveness, you enhance your own position without putting the other person down. In contrast, aggressiveness enhances your position but at the other person's expense.

Types of assertive responses: There are four kinds of assertive responses. The first is when you *rectify* a situation that has happened to you. Your telephone bill has an error in it so you call and tell them the problem and get it resolved.

The second is when you *refuse* something you don't want. You get a scarf from your parents for Christmas but you cannot stand to wear anything around your neck. You tell them gently but firmly that you recognize the trouble they went to to buy it, but that you feel uncomfortable with anything around your neck and would like to trade it in for a pair of gloves.

The third type of assertiveness is when you *express* your feelings. For example, you are discussing a potential new employee with you boss. Your boss likes the man but you have some reservations. A nonassertive response would be to say nothing. An aggressive response would be, "How could you say that about him? I couldn't see that he would add a thing to our operation." An assertive response would be, "I hear you talking about his competencies, but I perceived him just a little differently. I thought he might be somewhat uncooperative to work with."

The fourth type of assertive response is when you *request* what you need. Instead of trying to hint all night to your lover that you would like to make love, you say, "I see that you might be a little tired, but I need you dreadfully and would love it if we could go home and play." This last one is often the most difficult for people. Coming out and saying directly what they want is unrehearsed and feels forward. Yet, you will find that others in your life appreciate being able to fulfill a need you have and respect you for being able to state that need clearly.

Components of an Assertive Response: Empathy, content and action are the three parts of assertive responses. Empathy begins the statement with acknowledging where the other person is or how he or she feels. This takes the edge off of an assertive response. It is recognizing that you are aware of the needs of the other individual. The second part is the content part of your statement. This describes what your needs are or where you stand. The third phase is action, i.e., what you want. For instance, assume that you are working on a newspaper and have a deadline to meet (this incident has cropped up many times in writing this book). Your husband wants to go to a movie. The assertive response would be something like this, "I realize you feel restless right now, but I have a self-imposed schedule and the deadline for finishing this chapter is tonight and I just have to work on it. I would love to go to the movies when I finish the chapter."

The empathic part of the statement is: "I realize you feel restless right now." Empathy breaks the ice by showing that you are aware of the other person's state of mind. The content part of the assertiveness (I have a self-imposed deadline of working on the chapter and need to work on it) states what your needs are in specific content. The third phase is what you would like done, or the action phase (I would love to go to the movies when I finish this chapter).

You can probably think of a couple of times a day where assertiveness could be used. Try to develop some empathic statements of those examples you draw from your own life experience.

In order to be assertive, you must start from the premise, "I have as equal a right as everyone else." If your need is more dominant than another's on a certain issue, you would be surprised at how appreciative the other person is to know *what you really want and where you stand.*

The difference between assertiveness and aggressiveness can be nonverbal. It is important when being assertive to be firm and kind. Any intolerance, criticism or impatience in your voice or mannerisms quickly changes the statement from assertive to aggressive. Assertion-training workshops are commonly offered by private clinics or mental health centers. You may want to enroll in one of these to enhance your ability to be assertive.

Another example of assertiveness is trying to make your feelings known. Your boss wants a statistical summary today and nervously paces around your desk while you work on it. The nervousness of your boss is making you uneasy and of course you make more mistakes. An assertive response might be, "I realize that you are impatient about getting this report out, but your pacing around is making me make more mistakes and I would appreciate it if I could work alone until I finish." Said in a supportive, calm voice, the message clearly indicates that you recognize your boss's feelings, you have a need and know what you would like done about it. The results of trying out assertive responses will encourage you to do more of it.

Summary:

(Behavioral control is a critical element in building self-identity. Feeling that you have a strong inner core, that you can have an impact on other persons, that you can change your self-defeating habits, that you can assert what you want out of life, that you can set goals and achieve them all come through behavior control.)

Setting goals and assertion-training assuage anxiety. Instead of feeling helpless and out of control, you are master of your own destiny. Delightful anticipation of accomplishment and warm rewards from actually accomplishing replace anxiety. Your self-evaluations become more positive as you listen to positive feedback from others. You are on your way to success.

Part 2:

THE STIGMA
Prelude to Divorce Reform

The enormous guilt feelings revealed by divorcing and divorced clients in therapy mystified me. To take a broader sampling of the effects of divorce, I conducted a survey of the Georgia State Counseling Center clients who had divorced and come to the Counseling Center for services. Almost 99 percent of the seventy persons I surveyed reported strong feelings of failure in being able to sustain a marriage. "I feel like I failed. Something is either wrong with me or wrong with my ability to live in permanent union with someone else."

Feelings of failure lie deep. Why, when divorce is so common, is divorce so guilt-producing? Sad feelings of loss, regret, strain, emptiness, fear of new relationships, all seem a normal part of emotional separation. The additional overlay of sincere guilt about not being able to make the tradition work seems blown way out of context. Why? What do we do to our growing divorced population to make them feel so hopelessly deficient?

Long hours in the library, and in thought, produced a new insight. Divorce in the United States is a middle-class dilemma. Torn between traditions thousands of years old, and modern reality, the struggle is rather uniquely American. Other cultures have found ways to accommodate rising divorce rates. But not here. Attitudes towards divorce are hopelessly outmoded. We are futilely clinging to the past. Our attitudes are still punitive and unaccepting.

Why middle class? Both the lower and upper classes have always been able to find ways to ignore the binding of tradition. They don't care what others think. Middle class bears the burden of trying to emulate unreachable and obsolete ideals.

Mitigating the pain of the individual in divorce will occur when both individuals increase their adaptivity and the culture increases its sensitivity. I could not help the individual with divorce without helping society. Emotional and mental disturbances are derived from moral and value conflicts. Allen Wheelis succinctly summarized this point in his book *The Quest for Identity:* "Values determine goals, and goals define identity." Changing values, attitudes and laws on marriage and divorce are urgent problems of our time. We are long overdue for divorce reform.

Chapter 6
Facts and Forecast

Who Divorces?

What class of society divorces most frequently? Divorce would seem to occur more frequently among those of the upper rather than lower class. Members of the upper class have more access to divorce, i.e., they are able to afford divorces in other places and pay excellent lawyers to circumvent strict laws. Yet, as Karen Hillman revealed in a Master's thesis entitled *Marital Dissolution and its Relation to Education, Income and Occupation,* the lower class divorces more. Unhappy marriages are more frequent among poor families, reported Mirra Komarovsky in *Blue Collar Marriage.* Speculation in this same book recognized that economic deprivations, anxiety about the future, feelings of failure about not giving children a good start in life, produced tensions which affected the quality of the marital relationship. Affluent and influential upper-class Americans, on the other hand, were better able to cloak marital problems with mistresses, love affairs, country houses, separate bedrooms, travel or maids. Money buys many opportunities for greater freedom within the marriage.

The upper class can afford all sorts of opportunities outside of marriage.

Does location have an influence on the divorce rate? Geographical location does make a difference. The divorce rate rises moving from east to west and from north to south. Donald Cantor in *Escape from Marriage* writes the divorce rate is four times greater for the West than for the Northeast. One needs to keep in mind, though, that these rates are influenced by migratory divorces. If divorces are difficult to obtain in New England, persons will travel to Reno for six weeks' residency, obtain a divorce and return to New England. More liberal divorce laws in the West elevate the statistics. Religion and extended families characterize the New England states and very likely discourage high divorce rates there.

What about occupations? Lower-class occupations dominate the divorce statistics according to a U.S. Bureau of the Census report. Household workers, craftsmen, foremen, service workers, clerical workers and laborers topped the divorced list. The massive demographic study done by Hugh Carter and Paul Glick, *Marriage and Divorce: A Social and Economic Study,* showed the lowest percentages divorced were among accountants and auditors, college professors, draftsmen, personnel and labor-relations workers, physicians and surgeons and teachers in secondary school.

Interestingly enough, the U.S. Census Report found the inverse seems to be true for women. The higher on the occupational status scale, the greater the tendency towards divorce. Women who are managers head the list of occupations and divorce. Shortly behind managers were service workers (except private households) and craftswomen. In the professional field, the statistics for women were opposite to men. Female accountants, editors and reporters, personnel and labor-relations workers have outstripped the other fields in divorce rates by far.

Behind every great man is a woman. Remember this old adage? The statistics illuminate why. The consuming commitment of a professional job calls for a support person on the homefront. Cooking. Washing clothes. Transporting children. Arranging for baby-sitters. Ironing. Cleaning. The traditional role of a domestic wife facilitated the advancement of the executive. She took care of the time-consuming domestic, non-income-producing chores. The professional woman, according to the statistics found in the Census Report, may find marriage inhibiting to her occupation and may not need the self-identity concomitant with marriage. As the women's liberation movement helps to delegate domestic responsibilities more equally, perhaps the differences in the professional male and female divorce and remarriage rate will disappear. Marriage would then not handicap the professional woman nor facilitate the life of a professional man.

Does religious affiliation have an influence on divorce rates? Strong religious affiliation deters divorce. Catholics have the lowest divorce rate, Jews second and Protestants lead, according to Thomas Monahan and William Kephart's article "Divorce and Desertion by Religious and Mixed-Religious Groups." While divorce may provide an outlet for marital breakdown for a Protestant, no evidence exists that Catholics and Jews have fewer incidences of breakdowns. The means of dealing with emotional divorce may be the only difference.

Children? Do children help cement the bond between spouses? "From one-half to two-thirds of the divorces involved children, and in recent years there has been a tendency for the proportion of divorcing couples with children to increase," noted Carter and Glick in *Marriage and Divorce*. The percentage who divorce with children has risen from 45.5 in 1953 to 62.1 in 1966. More and more children every year are exposed to the stresses and strains imposed by divorce. If you look at the Vital Statistics Report which detailed "Marriage and Divorce" in 1969, you will find more than 840,000 children directly involved in his/her parent's divorce that year.

When Do Spouses Divorce?

How long does a marriage typically last in modern times? Are persons flippant about rushing in and out of marriage? The facts say no. The median duration of marriage, according to the document "Divorce Statistics Analysis" published by HEW in 1967, at the time of divorce was reported to be 7.2 years. Of all the divorces in 1963, only 13.8 percent involved marriages which lasted less than two years.

A casual spat does not lead an individual to dash to the divorce courts, William Goode's 1948 sampling of over 400 divorced women discovered, either. Divorces are preceded by a long period of conflict, and the final action is the result of a decision and action process that lasts on the average about two years; in the previously mentioned survey data which I gathered in 1974, a year and a half. Divorce does not seem to be impulsive.

Back to the stereotype of the divorced person. Who is the typical divorced person? There is no typical person. People who divorce are primarily people, not primarily divorced people. They divorce for reasons so complex, so numerous, so essentially unknowable that no one can catalog them and most assuredly no one can fully explain them, argued Donald Cantor in *Escape from Marriage.* The polymorphous world of the formerly married, as Goode concluded, does contain more lower than upper class people, more parental than non-parental, more nearly middle-aged than young. Morton

Hunt in his 1967 *New York Times Magazine* article "Help Wanted: Divorce Counseling," describes them as ". . . a world not of frivolous, hedonistic, footloose youths but of earnest, conscientious, somewhat harassed but hopeful adult Americans."

Trends

Since data were first collected in 1870, the divorce rate has ballooned in the United States. Nearly 11,000 decided on divorce in 1870, according to an 1887 U.S. Census Report, and this number leapt to 149,000 by 1922. Numbers jumped in the U.S. Public Health Service Annual Summary to an all-time high of 839,000 in 1972. The current rate is four times greater than it was in the 1920s and fourteen times greater than what it was in the 1870s with the population held constant! Just in the short span of five years between 1967 and 1972 the U.S. Public Health Service "Divorces: Analysis of Change," showed that the total number of divorces had skyrocketed by 38 percent.

Is this moral decay? Will this mean the end of America's greatness? Does this portend the death of the family? Perhaps. Perhaps not. Values aside, divorces are a logical consequence of several factors of modern American society. Birth control methods. Increased mobility. Softer living. More leisure time. Women in the work force. Women's sexual liberation. All of these factors add up to greater threats to permanency in marriage. We are speedily approaching the end of permanence in almost everything.

Urbanization

Agrarian no more. Over 73 percent of our population, as reported in the 1974 *World Almanac and Book of Facts,* now lives in cities. Alvin Toffler in *Future Shock* highlights the shift from an agrarian stage of development which has lasted 799 generations (650 of those were spent in caves) to a highly industrialized stage which has lasted for less than one generation. During that one generation, we have already catapulted ourselves into a "super-industrialization" stage. The last generation proved a crucial turning point in American history. We have gone from a relatively slow, stable, fixed, agrarian, horse-and-buggy society to a fast-paced, urban, highly mobile one. Automobiles and airplanes have allowed great masses of people the freedom to travel and Americans each year explore, firsthand, different jobs and lifestyles. Exposure to other people and ideas has grown at exponential rates. "The average urban individual today probably comes into contact with more people in a week than the feudal villager did in a year, perhaps even a lifetime," Toffler hypothesized. Constant exposure to new people and ideas multiplies choices. The isolated, safely-contained farm which housed a permanent family unit has dwindled to include only six percent of the American population.

The family in an agrarian society had an essential purpose. It was economic. The family unit provided survival. Everyone worked at an early age to ensure productivity on the farm. A birth in the family meant two extra hands to help eventually with the plowing. Death rates were higher and life expectancy was shorter. Economic survival kept members of families together. Each participant in the family had a vital mission, to help eke out an existence from the land.

With the passage of agrarianism and the advent of technology, the reasons for family unity disappeared. The theme in Robert Winch's book, *The Modern Family,* is that task orientation in a group makes the members assess one another in terms of job competence. When the task orientation is reduced, members judge each other on likeability. Winch observes that the relatively nonfunctional family tends to be an unstable family.

So it is in modern urban life. Nowadays, almost every basic need can be serviced by an automatic device or by local business. A dozen franchises line the streets waiting to feed you (sometimes for less money than it costs you at home). You can drop your laundry and cleaning off on the way to work and handily retrieve it the same day. Cleaning services send maids to tidy your house. Commercialized entertainment hosts guests for you. Dependency needs are spread all over the neighborhood, rather than confined to the family unit. To compensate for this loss of feeling of worthwhileness in the family, women are rushing into the labor force in droves. A 1973 *U.S. News and World Report* article "For Women: More Jobs but Low Pay" emphasized this by stating that in the past two decades fifteen million women have entered the labor force in contrast to ten million men. Results: diminished dependency on the family; increased opportunity to choose a desirable alternative.

Heightened Status of Women

(An even more recent development that pushed the divorce rate upward is the heightened status of women. Today women have more choices than ever before. Alternatives to remaining in an abusive marriage in yesteryear were almost nonexistent. The society provided few jobs for women other than housework, prostitution and low-paid teaching. Little status was attributed to any of these occupations except perhaps teaching. Lack of financial support, the stigma of being a female deserter and little preparation for independence left the woman solemnly putting up with an unsatisfactory home life.)

A husband could have affairs and mistresses and be

tyrannical in safety. Still, a woman's lot was better within than outside the marriage. "In the premodern world the possibility of escaping from a distasteful or intolerable marriage situation was very unlikely for a woman. It was difficult enough for a spinster to find her place in society; there simply was no place for the woman who had left her husband. Unless she had parents living who were willing to receive her or a lover with whom she might run away and disappear, the wife of even the most tyrannical, cruel or profligate husband had little choice but to bear her lot in patience, or to enter a house of prostitution. The law made it impossible for a married woman to have an income of her own," remarked Max Rheinstein, a prominent researcher in marriage and divorce, in his book *Marriage Stability, Divorce, and the Law.*

Women's liberation has extolled independent thought and action for women. The stigma of being a divorcee has gradually faded away. A new identity is available to women—being capable and self-sufficient.

Sexual liberation exposes another issue. With increasing status for women has also come increasing sexual expression. One anthropologist, Marvin Opler, found the status accorded women and the degree of sexual freedom allowed her were directly related. When equality exists between the sexes, so does sexual expression. Women in egalitarian societies are allowed opportunities for multiple mating, even if on a temporary basis. Opler in his article "Women's Social Status and Forms of Marriage" concluded that a double standard was more prevalent where women have low status, e.g., when women are given maintenance chores which have little monetary value to the rest of the community. As more women venture outside the marriage to sample what they missed in previous years, risks to permanent attachments increase.

Alfred Kinsey substantiated this observation in his book *Sexual Behavior in the Human Female.* Extramarital relations increased strikingly for wives By the age of forty-five, the proportion of women who had experienced extramarital relations was almost twice as large among women born in the twentieth century as those born in the nineteenth. A more recent study, "Sexual Behavior in the 1970s," done by Morton Hunt, found that where there had been a slight increase in extramarital sex among males, there was a marked increase for females. Women are fast attaining extramarital sexual equality.

What impact does this have on husbands? First, the prostitution industry is almost going broke. Prostitution in the 1970s, according to Hunt's national survey, is half what it was in the 1940s. I would guess that prostitution is somewhat safer than an affair with a colleague or secretary as far as not threatening the homefront emotional relationship.

Double standard no more. Only men in previous generations had the rights and opportunities of risking impermanence by an extramarital affair. Now women have that same choice. Emotional affairs on the outside endanger permanence for both men and women. Divorce rates will go higher.

Increased mobility, equality in sexual freedom, women in the work forces and loss of critical interdependence roles all increase chances of impermanence. American urban society paves the road on which divorces march.

Expectations of Marriage

The groundwork for the increasing divorce rate has been laid, so far, on a broad societal level. On an individual level, a change has also taken place which increases the likelihood of divorce—expectations for marriage have never been higher.

"Somewhere someone garnered the concept of a family living as a state in which two or more people live together in joyous tenderness and endless happiness. But speaking psychologically, there is nothing to indicate that anyone can be happy for more than small intervals at a time. We know, rather, that happiness as a goal leads merely to searching that ends in more searching," said Lee Steiner in the book *Romantic Marriage: 20th Century Illusion.* Two persons enter marriage with high hopes. "I expect my husband to provide support, money, lend an empathic ear, be a partner to my hobbies, provide companionship and sexual satisfaction. He should be able to complement me socially. He will know when I'm down and will anticipate the right things to say. He will be able to satisfy my every need, even before it comes up."

"She should be able to blend in with my family and friends. She should be intelligent, witty and socially desirable. She should be totally dedicated to me. She should listen intently and say soothing things when I am in need. She should fully understand everything that I communicate." If the partner fails on one or more dimensions, grave disappointment casts a shadow on the whole marriage.

Romanticized love and glorified images of perpetual bliss obliterate the realities of enduring tensions, compromising differences and tolerating maintenance functions. Few couples going into marriage are prepared for the shoals of married life. Each spouse resorts to habits learned during his or her upbringing. The ability to function adequately in marriage depends on receiving adequate resources in childhood. Resources are handed down from parent to child. You discover what worked for mother and dad does not necessarily work in your marital relationship. It's like having all the tools but the wrenches don't fit.

Our expectations have moved up on a scale of refinement. Up until this generation, the basic hard-core expectations were that the man be kind, a good provider and protect the family. The woman tended the house and family. Fairly permanent, easily-defined criteria. As long as the economic, safety and domestic needs were met, the relationship was in good standing.

The need to belong to a group was partially met by a fairly stable community and an extended family. Even after the industrial revolution, the paternalistic corporation helped satisfy needs for a tightly knit community.

None of these resources is reliable in the 1970s. The small four- or five-member family is the only unit left which tries to fulfill the need for belonging.

Even in the modern family, belongingness is no longer certain. Perhaps that was so in the agrarian family. Leisuretime hobbies, job-training, company demands and community commitments draw from time and loyalty once earmarked for the family. Conflicts arise when one spouse feels that the other is borrowing dearly from the account of family togetherness. Formerly, the deprived spouse could obtain sustenance from neighboring relatives or close friends. Transiency in urban life prohibits these close relationships. Constant change of home and job locations puts pressure on the isolated, recently moved family to condense and provide all of those needs formerly spread more widely among relatives and community.

"I have no one to be spontaneous with when you're not around." "Please don't spend so much time with George playing tennis, I need you to be at home more." Pressure mounts. "The kids aren't enough company. You just want to read at night. I am dying for more adult companionship." "I can't find a suitable group of people to rely on when I need them. Mary works nights. Joan and Paula are tied to their husbands. Please don't fall asleep in front of the TV, I wanted to go to a movie with you tonight." Demands escalate. Finally, divorce relieves the pressure. The too small nuclear family unit can't withstand the total weight of a husband's and wife's needs for identity and belonging.

Respect is another heavy weight demand in a family. Traditional cultures ascribe status. Modern cultures make you earn it. Traditional cultures automatically respected the role of wife-mother or husband-father. Husbands and wives dutifully respected the role of the other. Today husbands and wives have to manipulate their status needs with one another by enacting behaviors which either give or deny status. A complicated network of nonverbal interactions, approach-avoidance behaviors and verbalizations defines and redefines the status given to each of the mates by the other. The compliance by which one person revolves his or her schedule around the other's. The admiring look. The respectful tone of voice. The putting off of one's own needs in order to comply with the spouse's. Not disturbing the mate's privacy. Consulting with the other about a plan. All of these are signs of respect and status that can exist within a marriage. But, this is by no means common.

Yet obtaining respect within the family is more important now than ever before. Respect has become increasingly difficult to come by in an urban, technological society. You have to be highly visible in a society where the competition is fierce and sophisticated. A small group of elite people monopolizes respect. Over 90 percent of the scientists who ever lived are now alive. A small elitist class of experts consolidates the power to the exclusion of the middlemen. What little power is left is fought for by the majority. These middlemen don an "as if" personality. The "as if" person picks up sufficient jargon and nuances of manner to play convincingly the role he or she is in. The aim of doing this is not to do the work of the character but to develop an increasingly convincing portrayal. For instance, at a Space Center where I have recently done some consulting, the top level managers that I worked with were having difficult morale problems. Meaningful responsibilities were spread thinly over hundreds of high powered managers. Their talent, aggressiveness and creativity were being terribly underutilized. To justify the high salaries, though, make-work was created. The purpose was to look busy and "as if" you were doing something important. Underneath the surface appearance each manager felt a lack of satisfaction and fulfillment that comes with doing make-work at a high level. Edgar Friedenberg in his article in *Change in Higher Education* commented that the massive middle class is assigned rather illegitimate authority holdings.

When survival needs were at stake, decisions were life-threatening. Responsibility and authority were deeply felt. Social welfare now provides for back-up for satisfying survival needs. If you lose your job, you can collect umemployment compensation. The family will suffer but not starve. Middle management jobs, unlike the self-sufficient farmer, provide a more diffused sense of responsibility and pride in achievement. "If I leave, they really won't miss me much." The little family unit is once again called upon to meet these broader needs for respect, another towering expectation that could easily be crushed.

More recently, couples have been counting on each other to complement one another's self-actualization needs. Self-actualizing needs develop the inner potential of the person to the fullest. Creativity. Spontaneity. Autonomy. Realism. Emotional intimacy. Democracy. Privacy. Acceptance. All of these are inner characteristics of persons struggling for expression. Two partners in marriage attempting to actualize inner selves can be a complicated, refined and sophisticated process. Marriage that encourages self-actualization demands compatibility on such subtle but vital issues as stimulus seeker vs. nonstimulus seeker; social vs. asocial; political vs. apolitical; structured vs. casual; compulsive vs. loose; playful vs. serious; intense vs. flighty; emotional vs. intellectual; achievement-oriented vs. relationship-oriented; uninhibited vs. inhibited; and on and on. So great are the expectations that a discord in any one of the facets can destroy the entire marriage.

Trust, in this regard, rests on shifting sands. Any day the spouse can walk in the house with a new, unexpected tact. One couple in therapy is an example of how persons change within a marriage. Both partners began their marriage on a business bent. Each wanted to earn and save lots of money. Gradually, one partner became more hedonistic and existential. Trips became the goal. Spending money for clothes and a car. The underlying gratification to "take what we can get today, for tomorrow it may be gone." Meanwhile, the other partner begrudgingly handed out the money. Tensions developed. Resentment eventually dissolved the threads of trust, respect and later mutual attraction.

Let's take another example, a hobby. The husband disappears into car racing. At first, the hobby exacts only a small portion of his time during the evening. He adorns his hobby horse with new exhaust pipes, new carburetors, new valves. Weekends? Now spent at the race track. Hubby is nowhere to be found. The hobby is extremely pleasureful for him. He is meeting lots of people with a similar interest. Yet his wife has no interest in cars and prefers not to fake one. She only knows that he is no longer around. Car parts also eat into the budget. The wife grows increasingly dismayed. Leisure time has allowed that hobby to grow and blossom into a near addiction. Unlike earlier times, when hobbies were centered around the home (no transportation elsewhere), the modern hobby often draws the individual away from the home. The dissatisfied individual left at home eventually gives up. Another divorce statistic.

Intimacy in past marriages was an accident. Now it is a requirement. When psychological compatibilities define stability, the potential for impermanence is enormous. Survival needs mortar. Psychological needs blend. While it lasts, intense intimacy is beautiful. If it lasts, it is unusual. When psychological intimacy is a primary expectation, the chances for the marriage to crumble rise.

Tangible needs such as goods and services were basic to family unity in previous generations. In the 1970s the intangible needs are becoming more urgent—companionship, respect, love, intimacy, belongingness. This chapter points out the enormity of these expectations. Modern marriage places tremendous demands on its participants. Advanced coping skills. Sensitivity. Refined communication processes. Insight. Understanding compromise and fair fighting. Rational detachment when needed. The list is exhausting. No wonder so many marriages break down.

If your values are embedded in survival of the family unit, this chapter should help to trace a way out of the problem. If you are interested in a means to accommodate this reality, better follow the point-by-point suggestions given throughout this book.

Chapter 7
Dispelling Myths

Myths are unsubstantiated collective beliefs accepted uncritically by society and used to justify a social institution. Because they are so consistently inculcated in us at an early age, we don't even think about questioning them.

Legends about divorce imprison our thoughts because of the unfavorable associations with it. A recent White House Conference on Children stated that "America's families are in trouble so deep and so pervasive as to threaten the future of our nation." The implicit myth is that national greatness depends on the preservation of the family. Other frightening myths are passed through such statements as: "Liberalized divorce breeds marital breakdown." "The person who divorces is incapable of sustaining a marital relationship and needs psychiatric help." "Divorce causes delinquent children." These myths are emotional barriers which prevent clearheaded thinking. You cannot see beyond the stone walls. In order to gain a clearer vision of the total picture, it is necessary to look critically at the emotionally-laden myths. Are they true?

We may be locked into a system that isn't working for us anymore. Centuries of repetition have ossified these beliefs: the family is sacred, marriage is permanent, civilized life depends on the family. These beliefs gained such widespread support that people gradually found it impossible to believe that customs had ever been otherwise. The myths were created to protect those institutions from outside contamination.

The time has come to look behind these myths and deal with divorce on a more realistic and updated basis. Let's venture outside these walls and snoop around the research literature.

Myth I: Liberal Divorce Laws Breed Marital Breakdown

Marital breakdown, according to the research, occurs regardless of societal restrictions against it. Prohibition didn't stop drinking. It just sent it underground. Strict divorce laws don't stop emotional divorce. They just cut off one option in dealing with it.

One strong argument against liberalizing divorce laws was that, by default, divorce would be condoned. The fear was that instead of encouraging self-restraint, patience and virtue, the law would be encouraging self-indulgent hedonism.

Brazil allows no divorces. Yet more Brazilians separate every year than marry. Persons who have unsatisfactory marriages merrily go out and find another partner and move in. The director of the Psychiatric Clinic of the University of Brazil, Dr. Roueildo, commented when I interviewed him in 1974 that the attitude towards marriage is ". . . like a garden party." Marital relationships, he was saying, are somewhat superficial. Separations are not traumatic because expectations are low. The spouses negotiate the legal settlement in a casual court, divide the property fairly, decide a child custody together, and part. How Brazilians get around their seemingly strict code is told by Lynn Smith in his book *Brazil: People and Institutions.* The church does not recognize state marriage in Brazil and vice versa. Some couples will marry in the church and then claim their marriage null and void because they were not married by the state when they want to part. The church marriage provides a respectable, nonbinding marriage. Yet the country has no divorces.

Abolishing divorce does not abolish marital problems. "One needs but a fleeting acquaintance with Italy to see that marriage stability is not perfect in that divorceless country." Considerable numbers of Italian marriages are broken, remarks Max Rheinstein in *Marriage Stability, Divorce, and the Law.* Husbands leave their wives and families, wives run away, couples separate more or less amicably, not to speak of prostitution or the mistresses kept by married men. To be more specific, Rheinstein writes, "In Italy, where divorce until recently has been impossible, the number of marriages ending in separation or abandonment was in 1967 reliably estimated to be more than 100,000 a year." When society denies divorce, people find other escapes.

Desertion, for instance. During the early 1950s a million persons, according to the March 3, 1956, *Chicago Daily News,* disappeared annually. Actual numbers of desertions are impossible to pin down. Spouses most often do not take the case to court where it might be recorded. It is impressive to note, however, that in 1955 in Philadelphia, the number of desertion cases outnumbered divorces almost two to one. Clifford Kirkpatrick in his book *The Family: As Process and Institution* cited his research which found more than 4,200 desertions in the Philadelphia court records in contrast to more than 2,800 divorces. A high emigration rate into such countries as Australia, Canada or the United States in the nineteenth and twentieth centuries provided another way for thousands to say "bon voyage" to marriage vows. Up until recently, the repercussions of desertion were not all that bad. Sophisticated missing persons agencies capable of tracking down a marital defecter are relatively recent developments. The chances of deserting a family and getting caught in bygone years were slim. As that option dried up, divorce has become increasingly necessary.

When legal remarriage is not possible, people find alternatives that are illegitimate. Mistresses, concubines and lovers have always existed. During the late nineteenth century when the state of South Carolina forbade divorce, bemused William O'Neill reported in his book *Divorce in the Progressive Era* that the state found it necessary to enact a law regulating the amount of property a man could will to his concubine. You cannot legislate happiness. If a person is not finding satisfaction at home he or she will find a way out.

Migratory divorce historically has offered yet another alternative. Members of the upper classes could afford to travel from states with stricter laws to those with more lenient laws and then often return to the stricter homeland. Gordon Ireland and Jesus Galindez illustrate this principle in their book *Divorce in the Americas.* The book comments on the fact that Catholic countries such as Venezuela, Brazil, Argentina and Chile prohibit divorce. So the individuals who can afford it worm their way into Uruguay, where divorce is legal. The Montevideo divorce is much like the Mexican divorce to Americans or Copenhagen divorce to the Scandanavians. All involve the circumvention of the native law by merely slipping off to a more liberal territory, making mockery of the local prohibitions. Unfortunately, only the rich could afford it.

Migratory divorces, irregular unions, prostitutes,

lovers, desertions and separations constituted the main avenues of escape for spouses out of love. Strong evidence exists that assault and homicide data embody an even more flamboyant way to end the conflict. The greater number of all homicides in the U.S. are spouse-inflicted.

The tragedy of not dealing well with emotional divorce is brightly spotlighted in another earthshaking fact. Homicides, according to the U.S. Public Health Service Report, "Mortality from Selected Causes by Marital Status," were seven times more frequent among divorced persons than among married persons. Love triangles. Enraged abandonment. Jealousy. Killing the source of the pain finished both.

Chaos lies not so much in divorce, but in marital breakdown. Herein social scientists, legislators, politicians and social institutions need to expand their collective energies. How can we help stem destructive breakdown? How can we learn better ways of divorce?

Myth II: Divorce Causes Disturbed Children

Do delinquent children come predominantly from broken homes? Does divorce cause so much upset that children are marred?

One strong argument against divorce has been that "I just can't leave until the children are gone. I won't break up the family and cause them harm." So the parent sticks it out, not knowing whether he or she is doing more injury by staying or leaving. The underlying thought is that a child living with a single parent is being raised in an unhealthy, unbalanced environment.

While a healthy, happy home with two parents is definitely more desirable for a child, a paper presented by Judson Landis to the National Council on Family Relations suggests that a child is better off in a happy broken home than in an unhappy, unbroken home. "It would be unfortunate and unnecessary to write off more than two million mothers and their children as being shut out from a healthy family. Actually some broken families where the mother is the wage earner do a great deal better than unbroken ones in achieving healthy family life and producing well-adjusted children," summarized Elizabeth Herzog in her HEW study, *Children of Working Mothers*. A sizable study done by Louise Despert concluded that children in homes with much conflict suffer more than children in broken homes.

When divorce was a rarity, the child with just one parent had more cause for alarm. Friends of that child would reinforce the expectation that there should be two parents. Thus the child could very well feel deprived and strange. Contemporary classrooms are filled with children whose parents have separated and perhaps remarried. The child has lived through the process of emotional separation, divorce, custody, visitation rights and adapting to a new parent.

Children are more likely to be adversely affected by the feelings or manner in which divorce is handled. If parents and friends have a difficult time coping with the separation, children will indeed suffer. Friends of the divorcing couple may feel uncomfortable and withdraw. In Arthur Miller's 1971 article "Reactions of Friends to Divorce," Miller noted children sometimes note their absence and react with perplexity, turmoil, guilt or shame. Divorce itself does not injure the emotional health of the child. Hostility, jealousy, tension, destructiveness are the forces which harm a child. These forces can be as prevalent (or more so) within a marriage as within a divorce or single-parent household. The maturity and wisdom with which a parent deals with divorce ease the pain that a child feels. Arming yourself with personal skills which help you through separation becomes even more critical with children.

Myth III: Liberal Divorce Laws Will Undermine the Family

To the untrained eye, the astounding divorce rates (of course they were also astounding in 1890 when they went from one percent to two percent of the population) appear to corroborate the breakdown of fundamental family stability. Many people think that divorce and marriage are inversely related. If divorce is popular then that somehow threatens the value of being married.

Marriage, as an institution, is thriving. Numerically it has never been healthier. Hugh Carter and Paul Glick in their economic and social study of divorce concluded from their statistics, "In 1964 adults were spending one-tenth more of their lives as married persons than those of a comparable age in 1940." The proportion of adults in the late 1960s who were married was larger than at any other time in the history of the United States.

The moralists who decried divorce as a threat to the continued existence of marriage would have been shocked to discover, according to William O'Neill's extensive research, that even though the United States had the highest divorce rate in the Western world we still ". . . marry earlier, have more children and devote more of our energies to the family than almost any other industrial society."

Numbers of marriages and divorces, contrary to the above speculation, are directly related. Out of curiosity I correlated the marriage and divorce rates of each year since 1920 and found the two to be significantly related. As the rate of marriages goes up, so does divorce. Almost two-thirds of the divorced women and three-fifths of the divorced men remarry within the first five years of divorce. Most of these remarriages are for life.

The Need for a Primary Partner in Modern Urban Society

Marriage does not seem to be decreasing in popularity. The concept of the primary partner provides a common denominator for the various forms it is taking. Childless marriages. Living together. Traditional marriages. Open marriages. Group marriages. Pairing off (even in the context of others) persists.

Contemporary society in its complexity heightens the need for a primary partner. Although I do not suggest the best way of building internal security is to run off and find a mate, primary partners often fill the humanistic needs that society neglects. Such needs as feeling worthwhile and secure, having nonfragmented self-knowledge, warmth, cooperation, stability, affection, status, play. The competitive scramble that characterizes so much of modern urban life ignores these basic human needs. Close friends, partners and family replenish the supply. What is there, specifically, about modern society that inflames these needs?

Urban life and advanced technology fragment people in many ways. Insecurity results from the increasingly temporary nature of human relationships. The small community made individuals its business. Each citizen nosed into the sexual habits, children's accomplishments, vocational failures or successes, the hobbies of everyone else. The controls were tight but so was the cohesiveness. The community had a fair idea of what you were like with all of your many virtues and faults. Your tenth-grade teacher knew the subject matter she taught and probably details about your history, interests and family background.

Relationships today are much too specialized. The laundry man knows our laundry. The tennis teacher knows our game of tennis. The English teacher knows our competencies in English. The car mechanic knows our car. The psychologist knows our weaknesses. Co-workers know our job competencies. Doctors know our body, probably just one section (brain, eyes, nose and throat; gynecology). Each section of us is fragmented. Each fragment is related to a fragment of another individual. The number of people who know the entire you has dwindled significantly. And with stepped-up mobility, you are quite likely to live in a different location away from close friends.

I am continually amazed in a university setting how many students have no close friends. Over 18,000 students attend Georgia State University. The campus is swarming with students. Yet hundreds and hundreds of students wake up in the morning, relate to specialized teachers in class, return home at night, lonely. Each student aches for a new friend. Charm, personality and potential are not lacking. But the catalytic atmosphere is. Overstimulation gives rise to understimulation. "Where do I start with this overwhelming number of choices? Besides, other students look like they already have a cadre of friends. I feel fatigued just thinking about it." City life and large urban campuses preclude the constant bumping into a stranger which helped to cultivate a friendship. You have to be very aggressive or else you are lost.

Both fragmentation and anonymity provoke the desire to find a steady partner. One who knows you intimately. One who knows your pitfalls, your joys, your struggles, your history, your family, your needs, your dreams, your crises, your goals. The whole you. Having command over these modules is time-consuming and draining. Most of us want at least one person to stay current with our moment-to-moment vicissitudes. The community no longer services that need.

Specialization stomps out other important needs of human beings. Behemoth-sized corporations dominate much of our social, economic and geographic lives. Specialization means that most people are removed from the end product; job satisfaction is hard to come by under those conditions. Take a riveter, for instance. Day after day, riveting bolts on the fuselage of an airplane. The job satisfaction is found only in the paycheck every other week, in the knowledge that a person could hold on to a repetitious job and being able to acquire status on the outside with the money earned. The employee is so far removed from the total product that little satisfaction is gained in identifying with the end product. Creating the design. Planning. Assembling the wings, fuselage and engine. Putting the finishing touches on it. And finally, proudly watching it take its maiden flight.

Small businesses and shops used to allow for that kind of satisfaction. You made your own decisions. You planned for your own future. You managed your own problems. You exercised your own quality control. Jobs which lump together all of those facets are nonexistent today. Consider I.B.M., General Motors, I.T. & T., state and federal governments. Oligopolies swell the numbers of bogus jobs. It takes a herculean effort to make one's own opinions felt or to have one's efforts noticed. Even rapid promotion came to a halt in the 1960s. The end result: diminished importance of the job to the individual. And if you happen to be one of those who dare to try out their own business, your chances of failure are 90 percent. I discovered that surprising fact through a course I took at Emory University in 1974 on "How to Start Your Own Business." The Executive Vice President of the local Chamber of Commerce quoted that of the 400,000 businesses which were created in 1972, 90 percent failed. The choices are extremely limited. Survival decisions, controlling the end product or service, and creating ideas are relegated now to the technologically elite. Bulldozed into quiet conformity, the frustrated middleman or woman has little choice but to seek fulfillment somewhere else. One more inflamed need to bring home to the family. At least, the spouse notices you, occasionally, rewards you and makes you feel worthwhile, hopefully. You need to make an impact on somebody.

Companionship needs, spontaneity needs, self-esteem needs, family-rearing needs, sexual needs, community needs and socioeconomic needs additionally are nurtured by a secure home. As Joyce Brothers remarked, "A spouse acts as a loving anchor to the true values of life."

The family institution is not likely to die out. Supplemental institutions will grow up around it, though. Such institutions as trial marriages, single living, communes. The reason is simple. Our needs are now less linked to economic survival and are more highly individualized.

Myth IV: Divorced People Suffer From Psycho-pathology

Do marital difficulties have their roots in deep-seated personality defects? Some researchers say yes. Max Rheinstein says that marital difficulties ". . . can rarely be corrected in ways other than psychotherapy or counseling extending over some period of time." Edmund Bergler maintained in his book, *Divorce Won't Help,* that divorce and remarriage meant replaying the same record over again. His only suggested remedy was psychoanalysis, which would remove the character flaw which caused the original divorce.

As a therapist, I loudly and firmly disagree. If psychopathology is defined as nonconformity, perhaps these two authors have a point. Choosing divorce takes a tremendous amount of conviction and character. The person has to be strong enough to ward off these unfair denigrations. Categorically teaching people how to kow-tow to unresponsive mores is as irresponsible as the mores themselves.

Some individuals use divorce as an escape much as they would use other things or relationships as an escape. Pathology is certainly present in some persons who divorce. A smattering of individuals will go on and replay the old record in the second marriage. The whole world isn't fair and there does exist a phalanx of abusive, destructive individuals that roam the earth in search of answers.

Those numbers are minute compared to the vast majority of those who divorce. Some individuals who seek divorce are much stronger psychologically than the weak who choose to remain in a living death. Most divorced persons are responsible, mature, well-intentioned, loving individuals who are very capable of living intimately with another human being.

The blanket statement that all divorced persons need personality overhauls is visibly erroneous. Our culture exacerbates the harmful effects of divorce. We try to make persons endure an unhappy home life; we should facilitate the process of getting out. In other high-divorce societies, divorces carry no stigma. Divorce is not deviant in psychological or social respects. "Indeed the divorce system then becomes in effect part of the courtship and marriage system: that is, it is part of the 'sifting out' process, analogous to the adolescent dating pattern."

The first part of this section was designed to show how multiple influences set the stage for divorce. American society must bear part of the responsibility for increasing the potential for divorce. We should all take some of the responsibility for helping those out who get caught in its gears.

Chapter 8
Cross-Cultural Comparisons

As a psychologist who has counseled divorcing and divorced individuals and couples for many years, I began to ask questions about the monumental guilt portrayed by clients. Where did the guilt come from? Why to such an extent. As I have already mentioned I found in the small scale survey that I did that over 99 percent of the persons branded themselves as failures in marriage. I began to wonder what our society was handing down to divorced persons to feed this self-contempt.

The trauma reported by clients is not unlike that which society anticipates for them. The participants are expected to be unhappy and exhibit evidence of personal disorganization. If we hear of a recently divorced person who is drinking heavily, deeply depressed, dysfunctional on the job, has dropped out of school or is giving vent to anger with the opposite sex, we usually do not react with much surprise. The negative side is expected. The positive side is suspect. If a person reacts to a divorce with great adaptability, lack of guilt and confidence, we are less prepared to deal with it. Often those people are labelled as selfish or immature or uncaring.

I sought answers to these questions in the research literature: "Do all cultures breed this self-abuse in divorced persons?" "Is separation or divorce universally traumatic?" "Are there some better attitudes than ours towards divorce?"

My conclusion was that our society very likely creates a greater personal disorganization in the lives of divorced persons than other social systems. In order to find out why, it is necessary to explore how other cultures approach divorce.

Keep in mind that values give birth to part of the personal disorganization but not all of it. Given the normal disruptions of losing a love and established routine, how does our culture compare with others in helping individuals cope with divorce problems? First, we will start with divorce in Sweden, a Western civilization, very much like our own in having a Judeo-Christian ethic. Then we will consider cultures dissimilar to ours: Russia and Japan. The last two cultures display quite different patterns: Eskimos and Kanuri, an African tribe. Each one was chosen because of what we can learn from it.

Sweden

Sweden is very much like the United States in that the family is the basic unit in society. Monogamous, lifelong, exclusive relationships are highly prized by society. But their attitude is that since the breakdown of marriage already has deleterious effects on its members, the purpose of the law is to mitigate these damaging mental and economic consequences rather than augment them. The United States now has a minority of states which offer no-fault divorce. Sweden has had mutual-consent divorce since 1810.

The incidence of marital breakdown in Sweden approximates the divorce rates. Max Rheinstein in *Mar-*

riage Stability, Divorce, and the Law points out the direct relationship between informal and formal breakdown: "Once a marriage has ceased to exist in fact, Scandinavians, especially the Danes and Finns, appear to be inclined to have it also terminated at law."

Sweden evolved with the same strict Protestant heritage that the United States displayed in attitudes towards divorce. In the late seventeenth century, rare divorces were granted by governmental dispensation. Banishment from the realm, imprisonment, spouses of lepers, violence of character outlined the grounds for divorce. As the eighteenth century progressed, more liberal loopholes were acknowledged such as persistent refusal of marital intercourse, infectious disease, alcoholism or violence. The Royal Edict of 1810 added mutual aversion.

These routes, however, in reality were time-consuming and laborious. The most widespread divorces among the well-to-do were the short-road variety rather than the long-road. The short road meant that either spouse could disappear to a foreign country (most likely Denmark) and write back that he or she had left with no intention of returning. The divorce would be granted and the wandering spouse would eventually return.

The judicial farce of the short road was criticized not only because of its inherent hypocrisy but because of the advantage the affluent had over the poor. That kind of criticism was bound to be strong in Scandinavia where literature, theology and philosophy united in calling for truthfulness in all walks of life.

New laws were then created that corresponded to views which then prevailed in society. Sweden thus responded to the changing needs of its own individuals. Swedish courts today only pay attention to guilt when a unilateral application for divorce is filed.

The new laws sought truly to emancipate women.

During the early twentieth century, the Scandinavians decided to take a hard look at the equality of the sexes in the law and make some needed revisions. Upon close examination, they found that discrimination against women and the patriarchical system of marriage were so pervasive in their law books that they had to revise the entire system of family law. Major reform was accomplished step by step. The force behind this reform is encapsuled by the following paragraph from *Marriage Stability, Divorce, and the Law:*

> Their most urgent demand was female emancipation, above all, abolition of the wife's subordination to the husband in matters of family management, education of the children, and marital property. As to divorce, the demand was for a clean break with the remnants of religious dogma that had lost its spell even in the leading circles of the church. The demand was for a law that would no longer favor the rich over the poor, that would no longer expose the parties to the "humiliating indignity" of public admonition in church, that would instate truthfulness in the place of hypocrisy or a feigned desertion to foreign parts. Above all, the new divorce law should no longer aggravate the emotional and economic shock of divorce but should rather make it easier for all persons concerned—spouses, children, and even a paramour—to reestablish new, happier homes.

So firm was this belief in the individual's right to happiness that the legislature authorized, in 1960, state-supported family counseling bureaus. Here the couple could sort out the difficulties leading to marital breakdown and release some of the emotionality of divorce. This awareness program was intended to be applied in a reconciliation with the spouse or to a new relationship. The purpose of counseling was not strictly reconciliation, but understanding.

Conservatives might argue that these liberal divorce laws, coupled with state-supported agencies to help those who are divorcing, would encourage the disintegration of the family by facilitating divorce. On the contrary, in 1968, the divorce rate in the United States was more than twice as high as Sweden's. Perhaps we could learn something from their rehabilitative attitudes and agencies, liberal divorce laws, legal emancipation of women and abolition of hypocrisy.

Japan

Japan represents a country whose religious and social heritage is vastly different from our own. Instead of being divided into families, the social organization was based on groups. The basic cell of society was not the nuclear family of husband, wife and children as it was in Sweden and the United States, but rather the extended family and, more recently, the large paternalistic corporation. Religious heritage, likewise, was Shintoism and Buddhism rather than Christianity.

The house (Ye) consisted of several generations. Marriage did not require mutual love but dutiful obedience on the part of the wife. The husband, particularly, had the privilege of handing his wife a letter of divorcement and the marriage, as well as membership in her husband's household, was ended. Public authority did not intervene in the private act of divorce.

After World War II, the Japanese reorganized the formerly hierarchical social order and its base, the extended family system. The husband, wife and children were made legally equal. The institution of divorce was made public. All that was required was a written or oral notification of the intent to divorce.

Old traditions carried over, though. Family disputes were to be protected from the public gaze. Any disputes were to be handled in the intimacy of a conciliation council which, for the most part, excluded the formality of lawyers. Only those directly involved in the property or child settlement were to participate in the negotiations. The attitude with which Japanese divorce was pursued was one of cooperation, trust and fairness. It still is.

The Family Court promoted harmonious settlement of conflict while keeping the other person's welfare in mind. The terms of the contract were not spelled out in detail as in the United States. Japanese consider this practice offensive.

As easy as divorce is to obtain in Japan, the preference still seems to be for marriage. According to records from the *Japanese Statistical Yearbook, 1968* and the *American Almanac for 1971* America's divorce rate was three times as great as Japan's.

The divorce rate in Japan, Rheinstein notes, does not truly mirror the dissolution process. Japan has two forms of marriage, the registered and the unregistered. Marriage becomes legally effective when the registrar is notified. "Notification of the registrar may be delayed or never occur at all."

Attitudes towards the unregistered marriages in Japan are the same as towards registered marriages. Unregistered marriages, thus, do not suffer the same censure that couples do in the U.S. when they live together. When the mates separate in an unregistered marriage, it does not need to be publicly recorded as divorce.

"In effect, the Japanese system is the same as that of the industrialized West. But it dispenses with hypocrisy and thus provides straightforward mediation for that minority of cases in which agreement about termination of a marriage and the accompanying terms cannot be reached by the parties involved," notes Max Rheinstein in *Marriage Stability, Divorce, and the Law.*

Virtues which could be culled from the Japanese system are the ease of divorce, the unregistered marriage, the casualness of family dispute settlement and the virtues of fairness, trust and honesty which are extolled.

Russia

The Russian revolutionaries of 1917, influenced by the writings of Karl Marx, Friedrich Engels, and August Bebel, viewed the family in capitalistic societies as an instrument of exploitation. Women were subject to male domination. Under the influence of bourgeois morality, men were free to find satisfaction with mistresses, while extramarital affairs were forbidden to women.

"Women were also deprived of the opportunities of education and thus prevented from being independent. They were confined to the area of the household and the children; they had no chance to escape and had to suffer in silence even the worst abuse by their husbands," Rheinstein reports.

The Marxist viewed the Russian family as one based on love and affection; when the love and affection ceased, so did the marriage.

The Bolshevik government promulgated two decrees in 1917 whereby divorce was freely obtainable upon mutual agreement of both partners. The doctrine of love and companionship was left as a completely private affair. Illegitimacy of children did not carry a stigma. The distinction between registered and unregistered marriage became obliterated. However, some practical problems existed in that unregistered marriages were disadvantaged in respect to pension, social security, taxes and so forth. The equality of the sexes was demonstrated, though, through the fact that in a registered marriage, the man and the woman could maintain different surnames, choose his or choose hers. Divorce was handled by either party notifying the state agency. For a period, factual marriage (living together in the same residence) was all that was required to legitimize the union for the state. Likewise, living apart denoted divorce.

Stalin revamped the marriage and divorce system. Industrialization and preparation for defense against the expected fascist onslaught of World War II required obedience, patience, self-restraint and dedication to the state. Stalin reinstituted the patriarchal family.

Based once more on monogamous, lifelong, exclusive relationships, Stalin's concept of the family became the basic unit. Divorce was now based on a freedom to part from a marital relationship that, in spite of serious effort, had failed to be useful for society. The fees for divorce were drastically increased. The distinction between legitimate and illegitimate children was reinstated.

Max Rheinstein investigated the true reasons for the change in the marriage and divorce policies in Russia. A warlike country, he concluded, does do best with a patriarchal system where authority rules. Stalin was preparing for World War II. These pre-war decisions were extended after the war for another important reason. Population growth in Russia had slowed down to a snail's pace. Not only was the birth rate in the 1950s half what it was in 1913, but the war took an enormous toll in men's lives. In 1944, there were 50 percent more women of child-bearing age than men of a comparable age. The men had to be encouraged to remain in family life while also producing offspring with unmarried women.

To take care of this dilemma, Russian divorce was strongly discouraged but illegitimate children were taken care of by the state. In order to obtain a divorce, a jury had to look into the reasons and decide whether or not the preservation of the marriage would be contrary to socialist morality.

The end result of tightening the divorce process: increased "factual" *(de facto)* marriages and divorces and decreased "legal" marriages and divorces. Russians went on as usual without the sanction of the law. Those who decided to terminate their legal marriages would leave and move in with a new mate (known as irregular union).

These irregular unions brought the decisive motive for divorce reform in 1968, cites Max Rheinstein. In the years between 1965 and 1966, when the reform law was put into effect, the divorce rate pole-vaulted from 1.7 for every 1000 persons to 3.1 per 1000 persons. The backlog of factual divorces waiting to be formalized appears to have been enormous.

Kanuri

Let us now look in on a tribe found in the northeastern section of Nigeria (Bornu province). Richard Cohen describes the Kanuri system of marriage and divorce in his study, "Brittle Marriage as a Stable System: The Kanuri Case." The Kanuri have a primarily agrarian society. It is very much a male-dominated group. The older and richer a male becomes the more desirable he is as a marriage partner. The older a female becomes the less valuable she is until she reaches the age of forty-five when she is no longer considered marriageable.

The marriage and divorce system is structured to promote passivity on the part of the wives by providing them little access to the means of support. Their Muslim heritage restricts the role of the wife to the home and secludes her from the outside world. Marriages are usually polygynous so the wife can look forward to sharing her domicile with at least one other woman during her lifetime. Strict rules govern the relationships, though, as each wife occupies the role of the sole spouse for twenty-four hours and then rotates with the next wife.

With the rigidity of the relationships in the Kanuri system, the people still think that not being able to divorce is barbaric. To the Kanuri, the idea of limiting divorce or making it difficult to obtain would create an intolerable situation. In order to divorce the husband merely says "I divorce you" in front of witnesses. If the wife is living somewhere else he may send a letter. If the wife wants a divorce, she has to pay a settlement for her freedom. Remarriage is allowed right away for the husband and after ninety days for the wife. Children stay with the father.

Divorce in the Kanuri culture is commonplace. Six different Kanuri locations studied by Cohen revealed that the divorce rate varied from 68 percent to 99 percent.

What effects does this exorbitantly high divorce rate have on the social organization? First of all, it means that the household, not the family, is the permanent feature of the society. Children will usually change mothers with divorce but continue to live in the same household. The emotional effect is that individuals are trained to move with ease from one set of loyalties to another. This facilitates adaptation to the heavy losses that are experienced among warlike Bornu. Low level of emotional involvement with others also perpetuates the high divorce rate.

The Kanuri system of marriage and divorce disproves the myth that high divorce rates necessarily lead to social disorganization. The Kanuri society has maintained its same form for the last 800 to 1000 years.

Divorce is easily assimilated into the social system because provisions have been made for it. The society readily incorporates the unattached members into its social order through the extended family.

Eskimos

The Eskimos, according to Ernest Burch in "Marriage and Divorce Among the North Alaskan Eskimos," portray a highly systematized, yet highly informal marriage and divorce structure. Unlike the Kanuri culture, women are considered to have rights equal to men. The highly systematized nature of marriage and divorce is evidenced by the complex network of vocabulary with which the Eskimos label all of the members of both polygynous and polyandrous relationships.

The basic unit is the *ui-nuliaq* between a man and woman. The *ui-nuliaq* live together and have sexual relationships. In a polygynous marriage, the *nuliaqpak* is the wife acquired first and the *nukarak* is the one acquired second. Cowives have an *aipaq-aipaq* relationship. The cowife relationship is as vital and as important as the husband's relationship with both women.

In a polyandrous union, the first husband is a woman's *uikpak* and the second is her *nukarak*. The cohusband relationship is termed *nuliaqan-nuliaqan*. One of the most common relationships is two couples becoming associated with each other and sharing sexually their partners.

The most important relationships in this comarriage were between the two husbands and between the two wives. The wife-swapping that was described both by sexually-prejudiced American whale-traders and anthropologists turns out to have been a mutual exchange of partners. The event was just as much husband-swapping as wife-swapping. Both partners had an equal say. "As Heinrich has so clearly demonstrated, and as my own research has confirmed, the *ui* had absolutely no right to order his *nuliaq* around in such matters. On the contrary, the women had just as much to say about whether or not an exchange union would be established as did the men. Moreover, the women as well as the men could take the initiative in getting one started."

Eskimo divorce consisted of breaking the residence ties, i.e., walking out. Both the male and the female had that right. The marriage was not considered terminated but deactivated. Since remarriage took place when the partner moved back in, reactivation happened without much ado. The divorce rate was high, Burch estimates, ". . . there is reason to believe that the divorce rate (in the Eskimo sense) approached 100 percent."

Ex-spouses and new partners related to each other in a very structured and predictable fashion. The ex-husband and new husband were under obligations of mutual friendship and support as was true with cohusbands. A similar situation held for women; jealousy and antagonism were considered inappropriate.

Cross-Cultural Comparison

In comparing these cultures to that of the United States, we have seen a number of societies in which divorce is readily available. Easy to obtain divorce in all of these countries provides a means whereby a person can hold a spouse effectively responsible for his or her own behavior. If the wife were not doing her domestic chores for the Eskimo man, he had the ready option of finding a new partner. The Swedish woman who wanted psychological intimacy for marriage and was not finding it could seek another more suitable mate.

The difference in attitudes towards marriage and divorce in the cultures presented lies mostly in their expectations. The Kanuri and Eskimos expect functional behavior from their spouses. Divorce approaches the 100 percent level in both cultures. Divorced persons are also readily assimilated back into the culture. Emotional pain is minimal because there wasn't much emotional involvement in the first place and the extended family absorbs the detached single person.

Japan and Russia also have moderately high divorce rates but, unlike the United States, the social system is geared to provide institutional and attitudinal help to the individual who decides to terminate the marriage. As is true in the United States, people in Russia and Japan also marry for fulfillment of love. In those countries, though, when the love and affection end, divorce is available on all levels of the society. We still have not totally escaped our punitive attitudes towards those who seek divorce. More evidence for this is provided in the next chapter.

In comparing the United States with other countries and different cultures, several observations emerge. First, our expectations for marriage are not merely economic survival, but also to satisfy highly differentiated psychological and social needs. Likewise, we expect all of these economic and psycho-social needs to be glued together by romantic love. We have further added exclusiveness and permanency to the already excessive demands. With these colossal requirements for marriage, the pillars that could support it cannot sustain its weight. It is no wonder that the American divorce rate is the highest in the Western world.

Unlike Sweden, Japan, Russia, Eskimos and Kanuri, we have made few attitudinal or institutional provisions for divorce. We have had a hard time facing the fact that marriage can survive on its own merit, even if we support divorce. Sweden, Japan, Russia, Kanuri and Eskimos try to make it easy for a happy home to be reestablished where children can grow up in a healthy, undisrupted environment. Needed institutions and attitudes to improve American divorce mores are covered in the conclusion of this book.

United States' History of Marriage and Divorce

We have taken a rather fleeting glance at how some other cultures handle marriage and divorce. In order to fully understand the impact of divorce in the United States it is necessary to explore in greater depth our firmly-rooted inculcations.

The beginnings of our known moral development could adequately go back to the Code of Hammurabi. In approximately 1750 B.C. Hammurabi, King of Babylon, pooled, adjusted, expanded and revised older collections of laws and created probably the oldest law code in existence. Marriage and divorce laws, as evidenced in the Code of Hammurabi, had already become regulated by the state.

Family organization, at this early date in Babylonia, was patriarchal. Professor J.P. Lichtenberger in his book *Divorce: A Social Interpretation* described this early marriage as a "modified form of purchase, arranged with little respect for the wishes of the bride." The husband could dismiss his bride without stating causes. According to Section 141 of the Code of Hammurabi, as translated by W.R. Harper, "If the wife of a man who is living in his house, set her face to go out and play the part of a fool, neglect her house, belittle her husband, they shall call her to account; if her husband say, 'I have put her away,' he shall let her go. On her departure nothing shall be given to her for her divorce. If her husband say: 'I have not put her away,' her husband may take another woman. The first woman shall dwell in the house of her husband as a maid servant." The woman had the right to demand that her husband divorce her if she stipulated sufficient reasons.

Divorces in Babylonia, according to Lichtenberger, did not seem to be uncommon. The few marriage contracts and records which have been found had the provisions for divorce written in the marriage contract. The dowry was considered the woman's, so that when the husband lost the wife he also relinquished the dowry.

The Mosaic Law

Jewish law was derived from the Ten Commandments that Moses received around 1200 B.C. at Mount Sinai as well as the five books of the Old Testament which Moses wrote. Jewish law was strikingly similar to the Code of Hammurabi. Whether Jews were influenced by Babylonians or the two civilizations, widely separated in time and territory, developed a similar legal system is not known. The written law reflected a fully developed patriarchal family system similar to the Babylonians. Lichtenberger elaborates on this family system: "By virtue of his rank the husband and father was the supreme lawgiver and judge over his wife, his concubines and slaves, and his children." With dowry in hand, the woman at marriage passed from her father's family to that of her husband. Divorce was permissible for a male based on any reason but barely allowable for a woman. The Written Law, however, offered some of that same protection for a woman as was detailed in the Code of Hammurabi. The woman, with just cause, could force the man to divorce her but could not directly divorce her husband.

Christian Heritage

In 63 B.C. Pompey captured Jerusalem and the Jews had to accept Roman rule. Christ, who claimed to be King of the Jews, started the beginnings of Christian forms of marriage and divorce which took several hundred years to take hold firmly in the Roman Empire.

The Roman marriage had begun by moving in with someone. According to Rheinstein, so firmly rooted was this Roman freedom to come and go that it took the Christians several hundreds of years to convince the citizens that marriage was indissoluble. Marriage and divorce were both out of the hands of the law and under the ethical jurisdiction of the church. The court system was established within the church and the peculiar body of law known as canon law grew up to be applied in its courts. Unlike the punishments of other law, i.e. imprisonment, seizure of property and so forth, canon law used the fear of supranatural retribution. To counter the doctrine of indissolubility of marriage which the church enforced, a system developed which could invalidate marriages by calling them null and void. A solemn vow of chastity, existing prior to marriage; pre-contract; impotency; affinity and blood relationship, according to Rheinstein, were considered grounds for divorce. In the later Middle Ages the grounds for invalidating a marriage broadened enormously.

The rejection of the Catholic conception of complete indissolubility of marriage gained ground first with Martin Luther. Luther felt that marriage was a "worldly thing" which should only be shaped in the Christian way. A trend of accepting divorce began in Protestant theology and continued into secular laws. For Martin Luther, a husband was permitted to divorce his wife if she had committed adultery.

John Calvin and Huldreich Zwingli were anxious to condemn all different kinds of lewdness through giving the guilty party the right to divorce. Only Calvin, however, granted that same right to a woman if her husband had been adulterous. The "innocent" party was free to remarry.

Early in the Reformation the adversarial, guilt-producing proceedings for the divorce process took root. When the task of determining the guilt turned out to be too great for the ministers, they turned it over to secular authority. Civil courts were established in Protestant principalities of Germany and in other countries such as Scandinavia, the prince kept the power to grant divorce.

The thinkers during the Age of Enlightenment moved away from the church and the scriptures as a source for moral code and began to conceive of marriage as a natural avenue open to people in their pursuit of happiness. The highly educated studied the secular marriages of ancient Greece and Rome and discovered them to be much like a contract between any two people which could be dissolved at will. This new relook at marriage as a completely private affair which was designed to allow for the happiness of the participants was too far ahead of the general society, who were still clinging to the religious heritage. It took the enlightened King Frederick II of Prussia to introduce the new ideas of divorce before they gained widespread acceptance. The Prussian Code allowed for divorce by mutual consent, provided the couple was childless. No court determined the guilt or innocence of the separating spouses. According to Rheinstein, the Prussian Code of 1791/1794 caught on but was later repealed by German legislation in 1896.

The history of our divorce laws in the United States has been directly an outgrowth of these religious guilt-finding beliefs. In order to obtain a divorce, one has to accuse the other of adultery, physical cruelty, desertion and so forth. If some debate exists about the custody of the children or alimony then the compensation goes to the innocent party. The implication is that one party has to be "wrong" and the other party has to be "wronged." Sexual misconduct, for centuries, has been the primary fault on which divorce was granted.

The heritage of feeling guilty about not being able

to sustain a marriage is centuries old. The guilt seems to be a direct descendant of that time-honored belief that, once married, you were handcuffed by God and the state to the institution of marriage. Divorce was a punishment for sexual misconduct and a public court decided who had been wronged. Even with the multitude of divorces that take place in the United States today, persons divorcing still frequently walk around with this historically heavy yoke of guilt.

Chapter 9
Why Divorce Is So Painful for Women

In the mid 1970s we are caught in a period of transition. We have given an individual person the legal right to divorce and, yet, as a society we are unprepared to deal with the divorced as a social group or as individuals. We have given women the right to control their own biological destiny by providing birth control methods, abortion and divorce, and yet we are remiss in training women to be independent.

As a society, we drag our feet and refuse to acknowledge the need to rehabilitate socially a major sector of our population, the divorced. Our vocabularies do not even include words for "mother's husband" or "the daughter from my first marriage." People have no place to go other than friends and relatives to release the flood of emotions which surround divorce. The institution of divorce is virtually without guidelines, helping agencies, status or recognition.

Rethinking and reorganizing our system to assimilate divorced people is in our best interests as well as theirs. It is impossible to abuse one segment of the society without hurting the whole. Rheinstein set forth this same idea in his comment, "Dissatisfied people are the most dangerous to peace, political and domestic. Both revolution and marital disharmony thrive on dissatisfaction."

Large doses of guilt, shame and feelings of failure do little more than keep psychologists and psychiatrists employed. Let us take a closer look at what factors in the United States exacerbate the personal disorganization of the divorcing person.

Ignoring Rather Than Treating the Problem

We collectively pretend that divorce is not our problem. We offer no national day-care center support so that divorcing women can acquire job skills and reenter the job market. We have few known emotional outlets where the divorcing person can turn for acceptable, inexpensive, professional help. Little research has been undertaken to help understand and clarify the process. American society has no extended family system to reabsorb the divorcing person. To sum it all up: American society, unknowingly, adds to the syndrome of divorce ills.

Yet two out of every five couples divorce!

You may be asking yourself, "Why is there an obvious oversight on the part of psychologists and psychiatrists in not conducting research, describing and helping pull divorced persons from the emotional wreck? If dissolution is not only happening more frequently and assuming more importance in a transient society struggling with adaptivity, then why have we not provided nonlegal aids?"

One reason might be the oft-held belief that if we ignore it, it will go away. If we don't talk about it and discuss it intelligently, then it doesn't exist. If we provide no institutional ways of bettering the process, then we will insure ourselves of not encouraging it. Hunt's

"Help Wanted: Divorce Counseling" bemoaned the lack of provisions for divorce counseling in New York State Divorce Law: "To espouse divorce counseling would be tantamount to saying that divorce is as valid and moral an alternative to marital conflict as conciliation, and that people should be aided-at-public-expense in choosing and carrying out that alternative." Hunt observed that although New York legislators may have been aware of the need for divorce counseling, the danger of looking as if they were advocating divorce precluded support for counseling.

Another possible reason for societal neglect is that to many persons, divorce represents a morbid and threatening topic. Almost like death. Yet a larger problem is that we have not been aware that divorce has a constructive side. Over eighty percent of those in the author's "Emotional Survey of Divorce" answered that divorce changed them in the direction of being more assertive, more extroverted, more independent, happier, more confident and less tense. These same persons reported intense pain. For many persons, it is difficult to understand that something that causes us pain can also be a creative force in our lives. But it can be.

Ideals Beset with Hypocrisy

Our belief that marriage should be monogamous, exclusive, permanent and sacred has imprisoned countless people in bad marriages. Marital ideals have been set forth by national leaders (who had the best intentions in preserving family life) who seemed to have a difficult time living up to those ideals themselves. The middle class has been hoodwinked.

Indeed, our expectations and laws about marriage and divorce have been replete with hypocrisy. The persons who have been the most severely victimized by these illusions have been those of the middle class. That conscientious, hard-working, honest, middle-class person trying earnestly to gain society's approval.

The "Significant Americans," say John Cuber and Peggy Haroff in their book *Sex and the Significant Americans,* display a gaping hole between what they preach and practice. Cuber interviewed 437 upper-class Americans who set the styles and represented models for the rest of society. While they pretended that marriage and sexual chastity were quite adequate guides for the relationships between men and women, their *de facto* lives were very much in contradiction to this code. "Partly consciously and partly unconsciously, they have evolved a rather elaborate mythology which enables most of them to live comfortably with the discrepancies between their affirmed belief in the code and their contrary courses of action," concluded Cuber and Haroff.

Upper-class spouses have more money and therefore more access to an open-marriage lifestyle. The country home and city apartment afford lots of opportunity for extramarital affairs. Increased travel takes the pressure off daily repetition of a marital problem. Expense accounts mask keeping a lover.

On the other end of the continuum, the lower class does not maintain a strong commitment to values they cannot attain. Hyman Rodman wrote an article for *Social Forces* entitled "The Lower Class Value Stretch" which encapsuled this theory: "They come to tolerate and eventually to evaluate favorably certain deviations from the middle-class values. In this way, they need not be continually frustrated by their failure to live up to unattainable values. The result is a stretched value system with a low degree of commitment to all the values . . . ."

As one college-educated black to whom I recently spoke said: "Oh no! We don't buy all the marriage stuff. It is perfectly acceptable for a man and woman to live together without marriage."

"As a matter of fact," he amusingly commented, "I had one girl ask me to make her pregnant. She didn't want the marriage bit. She just wanted to be an independent mother."

Upper and lower classes alike escape from the restrictiveness of our obsolete marital code. Only the middle class is left to struggle with the traditional marriage with all of its chastity, exclusiveness, responsibility, permanence and constraint.

How does this make it difficult for middle-class people who are conscientious, earnest, honest, responsible but divorced? They have grown up with blinders on. They bought the belief that lifelong monogamy was universal and unquestionable.

Trying faithfully to uphold the demanding institution of marriage, middle-class people gained little exposure to alternatives by comparisons of classes in American society or other cultures. Families in America were not only the most preferable unit of society but the sole unit to be idealized. Those who left its rigid controls were labelled nonconformists and misfits and encouraged to hustle back into another marriage as quickpossible.

Self-identity, for middle-class America, was largely based on being tied into a family unit. The upper class had varied forms in which to seek identity, including family heritage, job success, travel, being a socialite and charities. The lower class hardly paid much attention as they frequently switched partners. Identity in the lower class centered mainly around survival. Both classes circumvented the sometimes suffocating demands of an exclusive nuclear family.

Unaware that other alternatives indeed existed in America, middle-class Americans took on the responsibility of carrying the weighty demands. Many dropouts of life-long monogamy with one person flagellated themselves heavily: "Why couldn't I make it in marriage? Marriage works for everyone else. Why didn't mine last? How could this have happened to me?" As remarked earlier, the most frequently expressed feelings in emotional divorce were "feelings of failure in being able to sustain a marriage." Over ninety-nine percent of those who responded to the survey reported this self-accusatory statement.

The middle class has been framed by upper-class inflated expectations and ideals and the lower-class inattentiveness to the seriousness of the marriage code. The end result: much confusion to the individual divorcing as to why these restrictive values work. for everyone else.

The goals of society and total fulfillment are certainly attractive. Virginia Satir, noted family therapist who has written several books including *Conjoint Family Therapy* and *People Making,* estimated that only five percent of the population was capable of sustaining this emotional interlocking of two people. The middle-class American needs to have more information about the probabilities of success of our traditional romantic illusions and goals. The goals are admirable if really meshed with reality.

Somewhere between our overinflated notions of the ideal marriage and our relative lack of skills in attaining it is the American middle-class dilemma.

Divorce Has No Institution

What is an institution? William Goode in *Women in Divorce* describes institutions as ". . . complex, interlocking structures or sets of role obligations and rights . . . they are both ideal and action, comment and behavior, aspiration and fulfillment. The institutional demands are not mere formulas. If there is a deviation, there is also a punishment . . . ."

Divorced persons move from a very structured,

strictly defined, fully institutionalized marriage to divorce where few ideals or expectations are found. The father is no longer clearly the father in behaviors. He is usually granted visitation rights but his paternal status is clouded. Mothers debate whether to cut off the father from the children or try to maintain a cooperative relationship. The ex-wife hardly knows how to greet the new wife. "Are we expected to be friends or enemies?" Friends struggle with inviting both of the uncoupled persons to the same party. The husband wonders whether it is proper to continue the friendship with his ex-wife's family. Neighbors hardly know whether to criticize or applaud the ex-husband's car parked at his ex-wife's house overnight. Divorce currently is an ambiguous, ill-defined institution.

Those things we don't understand we shuffle out of our minds or discriminate against them so we don't feel so awkward in dealing with ambiguity. Friends and relatives, creditors and employers, country clubs and social acquaintances, need to have a fuller understanding of the emotions and institutions of divorce to prevent them from discriminating against the divorced person. The Odd Person Out then acquires self-uniqueness and group status.

Increased understanding should help to remove the subtle (and sometimes not so subtle) kinds of discrimination against the divorced person. Credit cards for women. Maintaining membership in a social club. Difficulty in obtaining loans. Reservations about employment. Friends disappearing. Relatives looking condescendingly and asking, "Why did your marriage fail?" Added deposits for utility companies in order to get service. Lots of little ways which make the divorced person feel as if divorce has muddied his or her character.

Divorce is a major life event. Like birth, engagement, marriage and death. Lifestyle and plans for the future during divorce often alter their courses. Birth, engagement, marriage and death all have distinctive rituals, announcements and ceremonies associated with them. Each has a set of rituals to commemorate the event. The birth of a child is surrounded by showers, birth announcements and gifts. A wedding signifies the union of two persons. The funeral provides a vehicle for expression of sadness and loss. Death announcements and flowers communicate the event and caring.

Divorce has nothing. No announcements. No ritual. No celebration. No formalized means of communicating the event. Two persons pick up their belongings and leave.

The only way distant friends and relatives find out about the separation or divorce is by rumor or letter. During the divorce period, a person requires all of his or her energy to restore emotional balance and deal with survival issues. Explaining the whys and wherefores to close and distant friends and curious relatives places an unwelcomed additional burden on that person.

Birth, marriage, death are deeply moving experiences or events. We convey the message that our lives have been changed by a formalized announcement. When announcements of marital dissolution appear on the market and are freely used to depict another turning point in life, we will be much further along to full acceptance of divorce.

Lack of Group Identification

Another reason why divorce can be especially disruptive in the United States is that we have no extended family or surrogate group identification when an individual steps out of our conjugal (husband, wife, children) family. Cultures like the Kanuri and Eskimos emphasized blood family loyalty above spouse loyalty and the result is that when a marriage terminates, the two individuals have parents and other relatives to live with and be supported by.

In Sweden, Russia and France, the extended family does not absorb the divorced person but governmental agencies facilitate regrouping. Child-support and day-care centers are freely available. Counseling is offered through state agencies.

The Kanuri and Eskimo systems expect the formerly married individuals and their new mates to be friends. This continuing friendship provides more continuity for children. In the United States, we expect divorced persons to sever themselves cleanly from one another. Margaret Mead writes in her article "Anomalies in American Post-divorce Relationships" found in the book *Divorce and After,* "Another confusion in our present attitudes toward divorce and remarriage comes from our refusal to treat conception and production of a child as an unbreakable tie between the parents, regardless of the state of the marriage contract. In most societies, the permanency of the consanguinous tie between a child and its forebears, including the siblings of parents and grandparents, and their offspring, is taken as a matter of course . . . . People still seek help from relatives in other countries. But our present divorce style often denies the tie between the child and one of its parents, and it permits the parents to deny that, through the common child, they have an irreversible, indissoluble relationship to each other."

The small-group identity which once consisted of aunts, uncles, grandparents and cousins to fall back on in time of crisis, whittled down to the isolated nuclear family with just the husband, wife and children. Divorce reduces the unit even further. The single husband or wife remains with or without children, stranded.

We are slowly coming around to a better attitude.

Parents Without Partners is a group which backs up the fragmented family. By pooling goals, interests and resources, single parents are able to plug into a small-group identity.

Another variation on this theme is the "Pseudo-kinship" groups which Paul Bohannan described in a chapter of *Divorce and After* entitled "Divorce Chains, Households of Remarriage, and Multiple Divorcers." These pseudokinship groups are composed of links between the new spouses of ex-spouses. The former husband is a friend of the new husband. Children from the first marriage play with children from the second. Bohannan commented that children are the most likely to mediate these new relationships. These pseudokinship networks offer an opportunity for healthy, continued contact with consanguinous parents. They also provide a fuller, group identification.

Divorce for Women: Perils of Freedom

Divorce is not an easy process for any person. Both sexes undergo the same emotional strains and risks. The pain may be felt just as deeply for the parting husband as well as the wife.

Women do have some problems unique to their sex which compound these emotional hurts. Our marriage system was based on a patriarchical belief that women were to remain in the home and rear the family. The mores (values) of spiritual, selfless, compassionate, giving, kind, gentle and sacrificing virtues were ". . . contingent, however, on women remaining at home, for once outside its blessed confines they became coarse and unattractive," wrote William O'Neill as he recounted some of the problems of women divorcing in the book *Divorce in the Progressive Era.*

The conservatives according to O'Neill took the early view that this patriarchical, protective system of marriage ". . . worked to the advantage of women because they were so weak, or dull, that they could not survive outside it." Women tending the home; men providing the sustenance and protection. The traditional marriage divided the labor accordingly.

Early Hebrew morals applied the basis for the ascetic doctrine of inhibition of all natural human desires in the name of God and salvation. Lichtenberger wrote, "The early Christian Fathers held a lamentably low estimate of women and marriage . . . . The teachings of Jesus, of St. Peter, and of St. Paul were invoked to support the theory of woman's inferiority and consequent dependence . . . ."

Independent thought and action for women was considered masculine. Self-identity for a woman revolved around identity with a husband and home.

All of these stereotypes and myths have a place in history. For centuries, we have bought the Judeo-Christian conception of the inferiority of women and have fostered her dependency on men. While physical size and strength did provide a basis for this dichotomy in agrarian and preindustrialized societies, we are only now beginning to set woman on equal footing with man. In the whole of history, there has only been a period of twenty-five years, since birth control pills and more recently abortion was declared constitutional, that women now have almost complete control over their biological destiny. Thus, it has become practical to increase career opportunities and liberate the sensuality of women.

Freed from their biological prison for the first time in history, women are now caught in a period of transition. Many women of today are deciding not to have children. According to the *1974 World Almanac and Book of Facts:* "In fact, however, in 1972 the fertility rate fell to its lowest level in history . . . . This sharp drop in the rates resulted in a decline in the number of actual births ... in spite of the fact that women of child-bearing years increased by 878,000."

Instead more women have joined the labor force. Herein lies a contradiction. Today 40 percent of all workers are women compared with 31 percent in 1953. But the gap in pay scales is even wider today than it was in 1957. An October 8, 1973, *U.S. News and World Report* article "For Women: More Jobs But Lower Pay" reported, "For every dollar a male worker earns, a working woman on the average earns only 58 cents—down from 64 cents in 1957." These startling statistics which include blacks and whites underscore the crying need for urgent and decisive action to help women obtain education and career training.

"In 1973, women comprised 2 percent of all engineers, 4 percent of all architects, 5 percent of all lawyers and judges and 9 percent of all physicians," cited the aforementioned *U.S. News and World Report* article. In contrast to these pathetic statistics in the United States, Lee Steiner writes in *Romantic Marriages: 20th Century Illusion*, the Soviet Union women comprise 29 percent of all engineers, 53 percent of all professional workers and 76 percent of all physicians. We have a long way to go.

Because two-thirds of the female work force are in low-paying jobs, they have special problems in supporting children, in achieving career self-esteem and in affording self-indulgent leisure time. Included in these statistics are both black and white women. The point is spotlighted by the fact that, as a March 11, 1974, *Behavior Today* article pointed out, "the median income for all families with children under 18 years of age in 1969 was $11,600; the figure for female-headed families with children was $4,000." The inspiration that Mary Janney gives as head of the feminist Washington Organization for Women is that "young women will have to break out of the stereotyped job. It's going to be a struggle, but things are opening up in the nontraditional professions and it's going to be up to young women to push for them."

Women need more than just a nudge. They need help with child care. They need the hope of advancement in jobs. In order to break out of the inferior category, women also have to publicize successful women for others to emulate as models, women who are not just the wives of famous men. Women need more representatives and senators in Congress to give a voice to more than 50 percent of the population.

Following the November 1974 election, only seventeen out of 435 representatives in the House of Representatives were women. Out of 100 senators: None were women! The governor of only one state, Connecticut, is a woman, the first ever elected in her own right. The statistics are embarrassing to our nation. Women not only need the role models of competent, achieving women (and still consider them women), but also to wield political power in the national law-making body to speed passage of more legislation favorable to women.

Seeking and attaining self-identity outside of marriage is characteristic of a number of professional women. Hugh Carter and Paul Glick found the need for marriage seems to be less strong among those women who are professionals. "Both white and nonwhite women with graduate-school training who become divorced are more likely than less well-educated women to remain divorced and presumably to devote themselves to a working career." High rates of remarriage were found by Carter and Glick for women under thirty-five but very low rates were found among women in several of the types of work which were interesting and remunerative. Carter and Glick speculate that these women found this work an inviting alternative to marriage and childbearing.

Winch summarized these thoughts by saying: "It can be argued that the divorced or widowed man generally finds it much easier than does the woman to integrate with the nonkin aspects of society. Certainly in American society the occupational system links virtually all able-bodied men into a network of task-oriented interaction. As long as he remains in the labor force, then, marital dissolution probably tends to have less impact upon the husband than upon his wife."

Some attention needs to be paid to the psychological impact of divorce that is unique to females. Because of the inculcation towards passivity and letting the man take the initiative, women have very little experience with the feeling that they can exert control on their own world.

Emotional stability seems to be directly related to this feeling of being able to control your own world. When self-identity is based on being a wife and/or a mother, divorce threatens the self-identity. Women are then prone to increased nervousness and anxiety. Lee Rainwater sampled 420 working-class homemakers in four cities and compared these women with 100 middle-class women who were similarly occupied as mothers and wives. The results were reported in the book *Workingman's Wife: Her Personality, World and Life Style.* The working-class wife was differentiated from the middle-class wife by the following characteristics: She had helpless feelings which inclined her to take the world as given without feeling that she could change it. She had little interest, energy or skill to explore, to probe into things for herself. She tended to have a negative view of thinking. Lastly, she did not have deep faith in her personal efficacy.

Lack of emotional stability in the working-class woman was reflected by more volatile emotions. Less intense stimulation elicited stronger feelings. Working-class women tended to go to extremes to settle their problems. For instance, the response of a working-class woman to a husband's extramarital affair was typically to suffer silently or to leave. The typical pattern was that of passive acceptance rather than any active participation in influencing his behavior.

The middle-class woman, on the other hand, manifested more confidence about her place in her husband's affection. She took a more active interest in his career. These women appeared to be less willing to sacrifice their own interests in order to please their husbands. The middle-class woman tended to have a lot more emotional stability than the working-class woman, due to her feelings of being somewhat more able to control her own world.

The comparison between working-class and middle-class women was given to illustrate the difference in the evolution of self-identity. When independent thought and a feeling of being able to control the world around one exist, nerves are quieted.

Anxieties in modern women are alarmingly higher than in men. The comprehensive HEW study, "Selected Symptoms of Psychological Distress," substantiated this opinion that multiple identities reduce anxiety. The findings were derived from a nationwide Health Examination Survey from 1960-1962 on 6,672 examinees representing U.S. adults 18-70 years of age. Race, age, income and sex were all compared. The most evident difference stood out between men and women. "Women had significantly higher rates than men for every symptom." These symptoms included nervousness, inertia, insomnia, trembling hands, nightmares, perspiring hands, fainting, headaches, dizziness and heart palpitations. The study found that symptoms of anxiety were significantly greater for a woman staying at home than for a working woman. The difference between married and unmarried women on these symptoms was negligible.

Evidence that divorce poses a special problem for women is seen through the disproportionate number of divorced women compared to divorced men who have sought psychological help in a comparison the author noted. The client load normally is fairly evenly distributed between men and women at Georgia State Counseling Center (46 percent male; 54 percent female). Divorced women far outnumber divorced men, though. The percentages are an astonishing twice as high!

How do we help allay this unnerving problem? Giving women a choice to seek legitimate career identity is one solution. Also aiding divorced women to overcome the disadvantages of years spent at home. The handicaps are both financial and emotional. Careers are not the panacea for upset nerves, but having identity outside the marriage may well lead to more emotional stability across the classes.

The comparisons illustrate the special problem of a woman in divorce, especially a divorced woman who has not diluted her marital identity with other identities. A woman, I would venture, with self-identity based on her own unique accomplishments, personality, creativity and leadership outside of marriage would not be traumatized as severely as a woman with just a marital self-identity when a divorce hits. Men are no different on that dimension. They have just had more time to practice, more reinforcement for practicing and more opportunities to achieve self- and career-identities. The transition woman encounters special identity problems in divorce as she jostles for an equal chance in American society.

Part 3

CONCLUSIONS
Divorce Reform

Chapter 10
Conclusions

One of the most important values in American society, according to a reliable national poll, is family security. Above happiness, social recognition, honesty, obedience, responsibility, equality and freedom. Family security, by far, leads the pack. This Value Survey was administered by National Opinion Research Center to a national sample of 1,409 black and white persons over 21 years of age.

Yet, more than any other Western nation, divorce statistics reveal there is little family security in America. Somewhere between the high ideals and divorce statistics is a desperate need for change.

Where do we go from here? Three choices emerge. One is to treat male-female relationships more superficially so that a divorce is not an emotional divorce. Other cultures such as the aforementioned Kanuri tribe and Eskimos with high divorce rates encourage little emotional sharing. This, to my mind, is going backwards. The second choice is to keep the self-deception and hypocrisy alive. The list of catastrophes would continue to grow. The third choice, divorce reform, would first examine the discrepancies between our values, attitudes and actions and teach us how best to inform an increasingly large segment of our population. Intimacy in male-female relationships would still be encouraged. If divorce happened, persons would have some adaptive tools to use in coping with it. Societal support would help to sweep up the pieces of a broken marriage.

Let's fantasize about the third choice: divorce reform. How, exactly, should we go about updating values and attitudes? What would facilitate rehabilitation for someone fresh out of marriage?

In short: attitudes of rehabilitation rather than punishment. Concentrating on enlivening marriage rather than suffocating divorce. Respecting rather than ignoring divorce. Making room for pluralism rather than the monomania that exists.

Rehabilitation Rather than Punishment

Punishment in the past permeated our laws, attitudes and behaviors towards the nonconformist who didn't endure a lifetime marriage. Adversary law forced one spouse to accuse the other spouse of wrongdoing. The evildoer stood trial and was pronounced guilty. Only wrongdoing could dissolve a marriage.

The intent was to punish the culprit. Actually the process punished both. Adversary divorce law polarized the two into the victim and the tyrant. The victim suffered tremendously under the weight of being treated cruelly (supposedly). The tyrant went around with pangs of guilt piercing his or her conscience. Being out of love was punished. Falling in love with a third party deserved a lifelong albatross of guilt and societal ostracism.

No-fault divorce removes the quality of public flogging associated with it. On a deeply personal level, attitudes are still quite punitive. "She ran out on him." "He just doesn't love her anymore." "She was at fault. She ignored him much of the time." Look at your own temptation to take sides when hearing about a divorce. Society has agreed in some states to stop snooping into individual rights and freedoms.

Obstacles to human happiness and privacy are slowly being removed from the law books. No-fault divorce has changed the bias of the law. The right to be married is now accompanied by the right to stop being married. To show how youthful this attitude is on the part of society, we need only to turn to a 1965 Supreme Court ruling on *Griswold* v. *Connecticut.* Married couples in Connecticut were granted the right to use contraceptives. Justice Douglas ironically spoke of the ruling as a fundamental right, not specifically set forth in the Bill of Rights.

Up until recently, the legislation has attempted in many respects to control not only our minds, but our bodies. In January of 1973 the Supreme Court ruled that it was the constitutional right of women to determine whether or not they wanted to terminate pregnancy. Specific sexual acts have been customarily harshly punished. Sex was prohibited below a certain age. Homosexuality disallowed. Sodomy outlawed. "Illinois, Connecticut, Colorado, Oregon, Ohio, North Dakota, Delaware and Hawaii have wiped out some of these laws and moved toward legalizing all private sex acts between mutually consenting adults," reported Morton Hunt in the nationwide study, "Sexual Behavior in the 1970s." Our obsession with punishing all of those persons who do not fit into our narrow-minded notion of what is appropriate has abated somewhat. In the past, it has amounted to a gross abuse and misuse of human potential.

What ways do other countries rehabilitate and facilitate the functioning of their unattached population? The right to divorce without legal hurdles alleviates one problem. Japan, Russia and the Scandinavian countries ease the pain by making divorce casual rather than formal and compromising rather than competitive. Legalities might be resolved less formally and formidably in a family court rather than in our officious, sterile, blank-walled courts. Japan holds the conciliation meeting in a small, living room-like setting with flowers on the table and a gracious atmosphere around. The couple is encouraged to cooperate throughout the settlement. They treat each other with respect, dignity and trust.

Instead of judges, the court would have conciliators. (Hopefully, one of each sex rather than the primarily male judges we have today.) These trained conciliators would aid in emotional and psychological dissolution while the legal representative would attend to questions pertinent to legal separation. The therapeutic milieu would not remove lawyers from the process, but take them out of the quasi-therapist roles they are forced into now and allow them to process more efficiently legal matters.

Counseling would be available to individuals or couples who wished it. The purpose of this counseling would not necessarily be reconciliation but rather be a nonjudgmental arena in which couples could better understand their own dissolution process. Whether this exercise in cooperation was used in their own relationship or in the next one, the two parties would grow individually and together as a result of dissolution. The agony of divorce would be softened by a better understanding of what needs led into the dissatisfaction. And why differences were irreconcilable.

These processes would help for an additional reason. Right now, many of the individuals coming out of marriage drop from a high social status to limbo. From an intensely intimate relationship to a vacuum. The drop is too great. Counseling, whether individual or with the ex-spouse, helps bridge that rough period of transition. Emotions take a couple of months to drain before a new set of more rational, functional emotions can replace them.

Counseling provides an intimate contact with one other person who isn't making demands or judging you. A person with whom you can let it all out—without reprisal.

Preserving Family Security

For those who want and need family security, we need to concentrate on strengthening marriage rather than forbidding divorce. Forbidding divorce just cuts off one escape hatch. The estranged emotions crawl out the door anyway and head towards lovers, prostitutes, irregular unions, hobbies, jobs or anything which might absorb them. Who wants to escape a good marriage? Learning skills which are realistic and can actually achieve expectations will cement the bond between two people.

What kind of skills? The simplistic "Love thy neighbor as thyself." doesn't say how to love thy neighbor. The skills I am speaking of are intimacy skills. How to be sensitive to nonverbal cues. How to back off in a relationship when appropriate. How to express anger and feelings constructively. What expectations are realistic. The nuances of showing love so that it is well-received. How to listen. How to check out feelings with your mate. How to be specific in your compliments. The list goes on.

Given the best intentions and the greatest skills in the world, emotional divorce will still not be completely prevented. We cannot force people to stand still, they tend to keel over. Two individuals in a marriage may grow in different directions. Improving interpersonal and personal effectiveness certainly can save many of the divorce statistics we presently have (for those who want permanence).

Respecting Divorced Persons

[Two persons quite often divorce simply because they have two different sets of needs and gradually those needs become unbalanced] We need to bless persons and give them the lovely, precious ability to create relationships and sever them as circumstances warrant.

If divorce is a necessary step in the pursuit of happiness, then the freedom to divorce should be placed squarely in the hands of the couple. Respecting divorced persons means granting freedom to divorce and recognizing the special needs of that segment of our population. Currently the trend is to ignore or ostracize them.

I am reminded of the story where the person went yelping to the society doctor pointing at his chest. "Look! Look!" he cried. "I've got this terrible wound."

The doctor glanced briefly at it sincerely and said, "I'm sorry, I can't see it. It's got an arrow sticking out of it."

The joke is ridiculous but has a serious message. First we need to pull the societal arrow out of the divorced population in order to assess the real nature of the wound. That arrow consists of critical and punitive attitudes, lack of assimilating institutions, lack of guiding principles, discrimination, financial burdens and a whole plethora of inconveniences. This is just the societal arrow. Before you even begin to consider the raw emotional wound with all of its loss, grief, relief, anger, regret, defiance, emptiness and helplessness.

What institutions, you may ask, would help the individual regain emotional autonomy? An institution which delineates clearly how the participants, ideally, are supposed to behave towards one another. An institution which encourages certain desirable actions and prefers others. An institution which provides new opportunities, aspirations and fulfillment.

Provisions need to be made for those who comprise the league of the marital exiles. This book is part of a campaign that should be extended throughout communities to try to understand the problems that regaining emotional independence involves. Aware of the problems which heading a one-parent household entails, we should help create a positive role model for single parents. A role model from which to draw self-evaluation and respect. Cooperation rather than competition between ex-spouse represents one role ideal. No matter what the hurt, both persons would do well to struggle to save the friendship out of the marriage. Cooperation also facilitates the passing of the children between parents.

What about continuing relationships with the family of the ex-spouse? Or the new spouse or lover? In the aforementioned Kanuri tribe, ex-husbands were expected to become good friends with the wife's new husband. Likewise with the wives. Old family ties of the couple were broken temporarily and the couple reunited with new spouses and paramours included.

On the basis of links between new spouses of ex-spouses, this modern extended family concept exists on a limited basis in the United States through "pseudo-kinship groups." Phil Bohannan found in his informal investigation of divorce in the United States, that many of these pseudokinship groups have formed tight but extended family units. New wives are close friends with ex-wives. Children from both the old and the new constellations mingle. Making this an ideal rather than a rarity seems like a healthy sanction to encourage.

Another, more complicated, repository for trouble lies in teaching sexual ethics to children of divorced parents. The incest taboo has been a universal one and has always strictly forbidden sex with close blood relations, especially between parents and children.

This clear and powerful taboo made rigid what were spontaneous actions of affection. When these taboos are rigorously enforced the child is able to be freely affectionate, cuddle and relate physically to those members of the household with whom sex is forbidden. The affection is clearly interpreted as asexual.

Margaret Mead summarized this need for a stronger sense of individual and situational taboos by stating: "We rear both men and women to associate certain kinds of familiarity, in dress, bathing and relaxation, with carefully defined incest taboos in which the biological family and the single household are treated as identical. We provide little protection when individuals are asked to live in close contact with a single, closed household, with members of the opposite sex to whom they have no consanguinous relationships. This leads to enormous abuses—girls are seduced by stepbrothers and stepfathers, men are seduced by precocious stepdaughters. It also leads to a kind of corruption of the possibilities of trust and affection, confusing the children's abilities to distinguish between mates and friends . . . . The consenting minor may or may not be damaged psychologically."

As more and more minors enter households where step-parents and step-siblings interact without the deeply felt taboos, the danger magnifies. Confusion results as to who is or is not seducible in the house.

The taboos about sexual relations between blood relations no longer apply. The sanctions need to be explained and strengthened—with the emphasis on respecting other persons' rights in love. If two persons contract for an exclusive relationship, the restrictiveness of the dyad needs to be translated into the same vigorous sanction that the old consanguinous incest taboo originally was. Social mores should not be needed to back up every decision. Deep respect for individual rules and mores needs to be inculcated and enforced.

Developing a strong sense of individual and situational ethics in a child imparts the ethical nucleus from which that child can make personal decisions. The mandate "incest is forbidden" is not enough. There should be strict formulations for respecting and not encroaching on the territory of others (whether sexual, emotional or property).

Vocabulary

"No institution is fully viable unless it has verbal as well as legal concomitants," decried Margaret Mead when talking about the anomalies of divorce in the United States. If we are truly to make divorce a respected institution we need to affix some labels. The words "open marriage" gave legitimacy to the age-old practice of seeking relationships outside of marriage. With the words, open marriage, people could come out of hiding and talk about it.

How do you say the "children of my first husband"? "The mother of my children who is now my ex-spouse"? "The in-laws of my first wife"? And on and on. We, as yet, have no vocabulary to describe the relationships which result from divorce and remarriage. The Eskimos do. They have a complicated network of combinations which describe the origin of the relationship.

Let us play around with a set of words which begins to define some of these interrelationships.

Prima means first. The first marriage could be called prima-marriage. Children who were conceived in this relationship would be prima-children. The husband or wife would be entitled, prima-husband or prima-wife. In-laws would become prima-in-laws.

Seca (sek'a) would mean second. The second spouse would be entitled seca-husband or seca-wife. Children would be seca-children. Seca would precede in-laws, grandparents.

Tera (ter'a) would prefix a third set of children, tera-spouse, tera-in-laws, etc. Quadra a fourth. And on and on.

The vocabulary is only a suggestion. We need even fuller delineation but this division would be a start. At least it would condense the long paragraph of description you now have to go through to describe a relationship of a bygone marriage. I also like calling someone my "prima-spouse rather than "ex." "Ex" sounds as if the person doesn't exist anymore. Margaret Mead emphasized this in her statement written in her article "Anomalies in American Postdivorce Relationships," "At present, the vulgar 'my ex' is all that we have to deal with the relationship which may involve twenty years and five children. We should be able to do better—and soon."

Practical Rescue Operations

Reentry shock. After orbiting emotionally for awhile, the divorced person will decide to rejoin the earthly gang. The reentry shock is a bit much. "Where do I go to meet people? I really don't like the bar scene. Lonely hearts clubs turn me off. What other places are there that help persons meet the opposite sex?"

Both men and women experience this lack of meeting places which facilitate meaningful relationships. Swinging singles bars raise the curtains nightly on tremendously impressive male-female theatrical performances. Superficiality and insincerity seem to be the lines handed out at the entrance. I have known some terrific fellows and women who are at their worst in singles bars. Either nervous, awkward, pretenders or exploiters. Bars really seem to bring out the worst in them. The social set is to pick up whatever you can find and by whatever means possible. For the female, self-esteem is based on getting picked up.

The reasons are understandable. Bars force persons to relate directly to each other. The benefits are denied of knowing what you have in common with the person, what the personality is like before you get into the interaction. Thus, if you don't like what you discover then the situation becomes awkward and uncomfortable. "How do I get away?" This propels persons into a more superficial role where the real self is not likely to be wounded.

Indirect contact allows persons to sniff each other out. Indirect contacts are where you share a common interest and simultaneously can explore the others to see where your preferences lie. Tennis lessons, for instance. You ferret out whom you like in the class without rejecting a whole slew of others. The coupling is more comfortable, less painful and more natural.

Parents Without Partners groups pioneered the way for future organizations which stress less meaningful relationships. Established in 1957, Parents Without Partners states the reason for its existence as the goals of "working together through the exchange of ideas, and through mutual understanding, help and companionship which we find with one another, . . . to further our common welfare and the well being of our children." The direct focus on the children allows the single parents to meet and mix with a central purpose. This takes the onus off direct accepting or rejecting of contact with each other.

Sports clubs absorb many single or divorced

persons. Other organizations are civic-minded, book clubs and so forth. Primarily, though, divorced persons find themselves surrounded by excluding couples.

A club which emphasizes fun as well as meaningful relationships clamors for a creator. I have heard the complaint over and over and over, "Where, besides bars, can I go to meet people?" The segment of our divorced population that happens to be over thirty-five often feels out of place in a singles bar. That limits the choice for them even more. Some churches have responded to this need by creating divorce groups. Working through the divorce seems to be the primary goal for these groups. Supplemental groups to appeal to safe intimacy needs on a nondemanding basis would also help bridge the gap for the divorced person. Like a group which couples personal growth and sensitivity with travel. Or sensitivity and sports.

Full-Blown Divorce Reform

Right now we have a marriage monomania—the obsession with one idea: traditional marriage. Pluralism, in this context, would mean the acceptance of multiple forms of marriages.

Divorce reform necessitates more than helping persons pick up the pieces and enhancing the recovery process. We need to back up one step and take a hard look at marriages.

Young persons are nervously viewing their elders' experiences with unhappy marriages and divorces and are becoming increasingly wary of making any commitment. "How do I know that my marriage will not go on the rocks after a short while, even when my intentions are honest and sincere? How do I even know if my choice will make a mate worthy of a commitment without living together first?" Instead of signing a marriage certificate, the couple ashamedly lives together—

sometimes in pretense so the parents don't find out, and sometimes against the grain of the disappointed parents. Infrequently is the union blessed.

Both the parents and the children suffer. The parents think that their values have been rejected and the children feel guilty about disappointing the parents.

Another alternative: The young couple marries despite their reservations. A few months later, they discover that indeed the union will not last and they divorce. This time the couple is stuck with the expense, the stigma and the sting of a legal divorce. The legal process they go through is the same as a person who has been married for twenty-five years and has five children.

Parents are both disappointed and embarrassed. The parents have told all of their friends that their son or daughter has married (supposedly forevermore) and now they have to tell friends that the marriage was short-lived. Added embarrassment salts the wounds of the separating couple.

Take another example. One friend of mine, Robert, lives in a commune with his girl friend and another couple. Reared in a patriotic, upper-middle-class, loving home, Robert countered his parents' wishes when he chose to live in the commune. His mother had read somewhere that "everyone who lived in a commune suffered from psychological problems." She pines away with the self-blame of raising a son who has psychological problems. She has on conception of the fact that a commune can be another version of the extended family of yesteryear, only this time a self-chosen extended family.

Robert and his mother are both well-meaning. His mother wants Robert's happiness and knows that running against preset styles of living causes obstacles. She wants validation that Robert isn't rejecting a whole set of values which was handed down to her and worked well for her. Robert desperately wants approval from his mother but has decided that self-expression and autonomy must be a higher priority than sacrificing his identity to please someone else. "I really feel the weight of her unhappiness," Robert sadly told me. "It is a constant thorn in my side."

Robert and his mother want to follow ideals. His mother couldn't legitimately support ideals which were not handed down from a higher authority. Robert chose the ideals that were set by his peers rather than the going steady, getting engaged, getting married, having babies; the route that his mother had known.

We are at the point where we urgently need some laws to remove both Robert and his mother from the bind they are in. Society has moved from simplicity to complexity on practically every other level but marital relationships. Donald Cantor writes in his book *Escape from Marriage: How to Solve the Problems of Divorce:*

> The march of human thought is from simplicity to complexity. This is as true in the maturation of societies as in the growth of individuals; in the end education itself is only an informed appreciation of the complexity of life in all its categories. The law, therefore, as reflections of social growth, mirrors the degree of social maturity. Thus, when the law begins, it consists of simple strictures. The Ten Commandments illustrate law at its simplest level.

Other lifestyles besides traditional marriage have patiently been waiting in line. They have stood at the window waiting for the societal stamp of approval for decades. These restive minorities are getting impatient and are mobilizing energy to storm the gate of resistance and tradition. Who is in line? Mr. Open Marriage. Ms. Commune. Mr. Trial Marriage. Ms. Single. Mr. Divorced. Who resists them? Our laws, our feelings, our attitudes, our national leaders, our friends and our relatives, our ministers, our legislators, our corner grocery store men, our neighbors.

Traditional marriage in America is already being attacked on several fronts by these alternatives. We obviously don't need total approval for the different lifestyles for them to burgeon right under our noses.

Singles for instance. In his July 16, 1973, article "Games Singles Play," general editor of *Newsweek* and a recent dropout from bachelorhood, Harry Waters, remarked, "Of the U.S.'s 48 million single adults, 12.7 million are between the ages of 20 and 34—a massive 50 percent jump for that age group since 1960. The accelerating divorce rate has also brought swarms of young converts into the singles fold, where they now tend to remain for far longer periods. Indeed, the number of under-35's who have been divorced but have not remarried (1.3 million) is more than double the figure of a decade ago." This may indeed be one of the first generations which are going beyond seeking a mate to satisfy self-identity.

Communes are becoming a middle-class phenomenon. A February, 1974, issue of *U.S. News and World Report* illuminated this growth in the article, " 'Group Living' Catches on and Goes Middle Class." What distinguished the communes of the 1960's from the communes of today ". . . is that most are being established along firmly middle class lines. Leading the new life style: the affluent and educated." Thousands of communes are blossoming in cities ". . . as an inevitable result of increasing urban pressure."

Research Services at the Institute of Life Insurance maintain, "Careful estimates indicate that there were

3,000 communes in 1971, and an even greater number in 1972. Communards come increasingly from mainstream America." Carl Danziger and Mathew Greenwald, young sociologists at Rutgers University, wrote this study for the Institute of Life Insurance. This same institute in a 1970 study sampled the attitudes of youth towards communal living. They found the majority of the surveyed 2,500 persons, aged fourteen through twenty-four, felt communal living to be a viable experiment in living situations. The respondents were asked "If any of my children decided to live in a commune I would. . . ." Less than forty-six percent replied "discourage them because they couldn't possibly benefit from living that way" while more than fifty-four percent responded "encourage them because it's always good to experiment with different ways of living before deciding what's best." Still another sizeable survey of 651 college students from rural, suburban and urban areas discovered that eighty-eight percent of the respondents could either tolerate or accept family members living in communes. Mervin White and Carolyn Wells uncovered this youthful acceptance of communal living in their 1973 survey reported in "Student Attitudes Towards Alternative Marriage Forms." Among youth, communal living seems to be gaining in popularity. With a foreseeable housing shortage happening in the United States much like the one in Scandinavia and Europe, communal living takes on a practical dimension.

Women are also choosing to rear children without a marital partner to assist them. One statistic lends credence to this, i.e., 6.2 million women in America are heads-of-households as determined by the U.S. Department of Labor in the 1973 edition of "Women Workers Today." It may surprise you to discover that this figure now constitutes 14 percent of all U.S. families with children. It is also ". . . the fastest-growing type of family today . . . ," says the March 11, 1974, periodical *Behavior Today.*

Our already extant pluralism harbingers the imminent demise of traditional marriage as the only choice in lifestyles. Pluralism is a condition of society in which numerous distinct ethnic, religious or cultural groups coexist peacefully within one nation. Persons would be allowed to be married to marriage (traditional marriage) and married to each other (trial marriage). We have the computers, the technology, the communication devices to accommodate various lifestyles within our country.

Education in California already has made a major breakthrough in pluralism. *Footnotes to the Future* (volume 4, number 7) exclaimed, "In several California communities, public schools now offer three program options—open, middle ground and conservative—so that parents can choose the type of classroom and education they want for their children. The conservative alternative offers tightly structured, sequential learning systems, the development of basic academic skills, strict discipline, dress codes, citizenship, respect, personal responsibility, ABC grading systems, competition." Implicit in the concept of pluralism is the genuine respect for each other's right to be different, but equal.

Societal approbation of different lifestyles will go a long way in helping individuals make meaningful choices. Your sister, for instance, decides to opt for a traditional, authoritarian marriage where the husband is the boss and she obediently serves him. You, on the other hand, prefer an egalitarian relationship with several persons so you choose a commune. A pluralistic society is one in which both choices are perfectly acceptable. What is validated and respected is not the content of the decision (traditional marriage or communal living), but your right to choose.

One of the common denominators in marital difficulties is inability to tolerate differences in the mate. By setting an example of tolerance on a societal level and legally making room for different lifestyles, individuals become more broad-minded.

Contract Marriages

We need a legal vehicle for pluralism. Margaret Mead has espoused one vehicle with which pluralism would be legitimized, i.e., contract marriages. With contract marriages, or trial marriages, you could write your own legal contract and level of commitment into the marriage. Two or more persons legally and publicly would announce the mutual pledge. Central issues, i.e., duration of the contract, division of property and surname choice would be stipulated in the contract. Example: a couple could determine that they wanted a three-year marriage with communal property yet each wanted to retain his or her own surname.

Peter and Martha, for example, desire full commitment to each other but without children. Martha has a professional identity so she prefers to keep her own name. Both partners feel that a three-year contract would give them enough time to decide whether or not they wanted to go on from there. The two draw up their contract in a small state registrar's office with a marriage-contract clerk. Three years pass. Peter and Martha have to renew their contract in order for it to be legally binding. The marriage would then be accompanied by a ceremony (if desired) to celebrate the union with friends and relatives.

At the end of three years, Peter and Martha could opt for traditional marriage, could say good-bye to each other or they could renew the contract for a specified period of time.

With contract marriages available along with traditional marriage, there are a number of advantages. First, the individual has more choices. Second, legal entanglements in contract marriage are at a minimal level. Relationships are created and dissolved more easily. Third, couples living together today would have a legal and social means of expressing their relationship.

The age-old question arises: "What would you do with children who are born from this impermanent union?" First, the birth control pill has knocked the wind out of this argument. Couples have total control over family planning. Abortion is available for those whom contraception has failed. Thus, for the first time in history, couples are truly allowed to mate free from the biological consequences.

I have heard this sentence from several divorced clients, "I thought if we had a child that it would take care of our marital problems. The marriage was shaky and I thought that having children would stabilize it." Of course, it didn't. While having two forms of marital commitment would not completely circumvent divorces, the seriousness of the divorce would be commensurate with the seriousness of the marital contract. Expectations of friends, relatives and employers would not be as thwarted in the dissolution of a contract marriage as in the dissolution of a traditional marriage.

What about disputes over property at the end of the contract? A trained conciliator would help if problems arose.

The whole concept of divorce in a contract marriage would be changed. Built into the contract is an expected expiration date. Unless the couple keeps the relationship vital and satisfying, the contract would not be renewed. Dissolution is automatic, unless a concerted effort is made to visit the registrar and regenerate the commitment.

Summary

Just like divorce, this book is a beginning and not the end. A vast social effort needs to be made which further explores and ameliorates the welfare of persons caught outside of the traditional marriage fortress.

The purpose of this treatise is not to invalidate ideals for relationships but to diversify them. Traditional marriage is not being dethroned but rather asked to share its crown with other covenants. The Single. The Commune. The Family. The Divorced. The Partners. Each sacred in its own right. Each with a legal vehicle which carries respect and expresses its own purposes. Only then can we reduce the number of casualties of persons who feel self-contempt because they don't fit the narrow definition of the right way. For instance, the children who feel condemned and misunderstood by parents because they are living with a member of the opposite sex. Divorced persons who feel that they have failed because they couldn't sustain a lifelong marriage. Married persons who unhappily submit to ulcers, nervous breakdowns, migraine headaches and so forth, because they are too afraid to try again.

For the individual, divorce can be a brutalizing experience. Yes, it hurts when divorce jabs you into new awareness and realities. Divorced persons, though, who have learned to use their pain to further their own growth often report at the end, "It was the best thing that ever happened to me."

Self-improvement in divorce, however, will be hamstrung unless society drops its branding iron. Divorce does not mean the participant is immature or irresponsible. Often divorce is the most responsible decision a person can make.

Dropping the branding iron involves shifting societal attitudes. From punitive to rehabilitative. From monomania (obsession with traditional marriage) to pluralism. From ignoring divorce as an institution to understanding its process and dealing with it respectfully.

Only then can we march forward into the future instead of backward.

Bibliography

APA Monitor. "Homosexuality dropped as mental disorder." Volume 4, Number 2:1, February, 1974.

Baker, Luther G. "The personal and social adjustment of the never-married woman." *Journal of Marriage and the Family.* Volume 30, Number 3:473-479, August, 1968.

Bandura, Albert. *Principles of Behavior Modification.* New York: Holt, 1969.

Behavior Today. "The female headed family." Volume 5, Number 10:70-71, March 11, 1974.

Belcher, John C. "The one-person household: a consequence of the isolated nuclear family?" *Journal of Marriage and the Family.* Volume 29, Number 3:534-540, August, 1967.

Bergler, Edmund. *Divorce Won't Help.* New York: Harper, 1948.

Bernard, Jessie. "No news, but new ideas." In Paul Bohannan, ed., *Divorce and After,* New York: Doubleday Anchor, 1971. Pp. 3-32.

Blake, Wilson Manfred. *The Road to Reno.* New York: Bantam, 1972.

Bohannan, Paul, ed. *Divorce and After: An Analysis of the Emotional and Social Problems of Divorce.* New York: Doubleday Anchor, 1971.

Bohannan, Paul. "Divorce chains, households of remarriage, and multiple divorces." *Divorce and After.* New York: Doubleday Anchor, 1971. Pp. 127-142.

Bohannan, Paul. "The six stations of divorce." *Divorce and After.* New York: Doubleday Anchor, 1971. Pp. 33-62.

Bohannan, Paul. "Some thoughts on divorce reform" *Divorce and After.* New York: Doubleday Anchor, 1971. Pp. 283-300.

Bowlby, John. *Separation: Anxiety and Anger.* New York: Basic Books, 1973.

Brothers, Joyce. *Brothers' System for Liberated Love and Marriage.* New York: Wyden, 1972.

Burch, Ernest S., Jr. "Marriage and divorce among the North Alaskan Eskimos." *Divorce and After.*, ed. Paul Bohannan. New York: Doubleday Anchor, 1971.

Burgess, Ernest W. and Wallin, Paul. "Homogamy in social characteristics." *The American Journal of Sociology.* Volume XLIX, Number 2:109-124, September, 1943.

Caird, Mona. *The Morality of Marriage.* London: George Redway, 1897.

Cammer, Leonard, M.D. *Up From Depression.* New York: Pocket Books, 1971.

Cantor, Donald J. *Escape from Marriage: How to Solve the Problems of Divorce.* New York: William Morrow, 1971.

Carter, Hugh. "Eight myths about divorce—and the facts." In *Search for Human Understanding: A Reader in Psychology,* ed. Michael Merbaum and George Strickler. New York: Holt, 1971.

Carter, Hugh and Glick, Paul C. *Marriage and Divorce: A Social and Economic Study.* Cambridge, Mass.: Harvard University Press, 1970.

Chesler, Phylis. *Women and Madness.* New York: Avon, 1972.

Chester, Robert and Streather, Jane. "Cruelty in English divorce: some empirical findings." *Journal of Marriage and the Family.* Volume 34, Number 4:706-712, November, 1972.

Clements, William H. "Marital interaction and marital stability: a point of view and a descriptive comparison of stable and unstable marriages." *Journal of Marriage and the Family.* Volume 29, Number 4:697-702, November, 1967.

Cohen, Ronald. "Brittle marriage as a stable system: the Kanuri case." In *Divorce and After,* ed. Paul Bohannan. New York: Doubleday Anchor 1971. Pp. 205-242.

Cooper, David. *The Death of the Family.* New York: Random House, 1970.

Costello, Charles. *Symptoms of Psychopathology: A Handbook.* New York: John Wiley, 1970.

Crouse, Bryant; Karlins, Marvin; and Schroder, Harold. "Conceptual complexity and marital happiness." *Journal of Marriage and the Family.* Volume 30, Number 4:643-646, November, 1968.

Cuber, John F. and Haroff, Peggy. *The Significant Americans: A Study of Sexual Behavior Among The Affluent.* New York: Appleton-Century, 1965.

Cutright, Phillips. "Income and family events: marital stability." *Journal of Marriage and the Family.* Volume 33, Number 2:291-306, May, 1971.

Danziger, Carl and Greenwald, Mathew. *Alternatives: A Look at Unmarried Couples and Communes.* New York: Institute of Life Insurance Research Services, 1973.

Despert, J. Louise. *Children of Divorce.* New York: Doubleday, 1953.

DeWolf, Rose. *The Bonds of Acrimony.* New York: Lippincott, 1970.

Donelson, Kenneth and Irene. *Married Today and Single Tomorrow: Marriage Breakup and the Law.* New York: Doubleday, 1969.

Ellis, Albert. *Reason and Emotion in Psychotherapy.* New York: Lyle Stuart, 1962.

Ellis, Albert, Ph.D and Harper, Robert A. *A Guide to Rational Living.* Englewood Cliffs, New Jersey: Prentice-Hall, 1961.

Ellis, Albert and Harper, Robert A. *Creative Marriage.* New York: Lyle Stuart, 1961.

Erikson, Erik H. *Identity: Youth and Crisis.* New York: Norton, 1968.

Fenelon, Bill. "State variations in the United States divorce rates." *Journal of Marriage and the Family.* Volume 33, Number 2:321-327, May, 1971.

Foa, Uriel G. and Donnenwerth, Gregory V. "Love poverty in modern culture and sensitivity training." *Sociological Inquiry.* Volume 41, Number 2:149-159 Spring, 1971.

Footnotes to the Future. "Back to the three r's." Volume 4, Number 2, February, 1974.

Friedenberg, Edgar Z. "The revolt against democracy." *Changes in Higher Education.* Volume 1, Number 3:11-18, May-June, 1969.

Frohlich, Newton. *Making the Best of It: A Common Sense Guide to Negotiating a Divorce.* New York: Harper, 1971.

Fromm, Erich. *The Anatomy of Human Destructiveness.* New York: Holt, 1973.

Fromm, Erich. *Man for Himself: An Inquiry into the Psychology of Human Ethics.* Greenwich, Connecticut: Fawcett, 1947.

Glasser, Paul H. and Glasser, Lois N. *Families in Crisis.* New York: Harper, 1970.

Gebhard, Paul. "Postmarital coitus among widows and divorcees." In *Divorce and After,* ed. Paul Bohannan. New York: Doubleday Anchor, 1971.

Glick, Paul C. and Norton, Arthur J. "Frequency, duration, and probability of marriage and divorce." *Journal of Marriage and the Family.* Volume 33, Number 2:307-317, May 1971.

Goldfried, Marvin R. and Merbaum, Michael. *Behavior Change Through Self-Control.* New York: Holt, 1973.

Goode, William J. "Marital satisfaction and instability: a cross-cultural analysis of divorce rates." In *Families in Crisis,* ed. Paul Glasser and Lois Glasser. New York: Harper, 1970. P. 154.

Goode, William. *Women in Divorce.* New York: Free Press, 1956.

Goodman, Norman and Ofshe, Richard. "Empathy, communication, efficiency and marital status."

Journal of Marriage and the Family. Volume 30, Number 4:597-603, November, 1968.

Gordon, Michael. *The Nuclear Family in Crisis: The Search for an Alternative.* New York: Harper and Row, 1972.

Gordon, Thomas. *Parent Effectiveness Training.* New York: Peter Wyden, 1971.

Gurin, Gerald; Veroff, Joseph; and Feld, Sheila. *Americans View Their Mental Health.* Joint Commission on Mental Illness and Health, Monograph Series number 4. New York: Basic Books, 1960.

Gurr, Ted. "Psychological factors in civil violence." *World Politics.* Volume 20, Number 2:245-278, January, 1968.

Hawkins, James. "Associations between companionship, hostility, and marital satisfaction." *Journal of Marriage and the Family.* Volume 30, Number 4:647-650, November, 1968.

Heinicke, Christoph S. Westheimer I. *Brief Separations.* New York: International Universities Press, 1966.

Herzog, Elizabeth. *Children of Working Mothers.* U.S. Department of Health, Education and Welfare Children's Bureau, Publication Number 382-1960, Social Security Administration, Children's Bureau, 1960. U.S. Government Printing Office, Washington, D.C.

Hillman, Karen G. "Marital dissolution and its relation to education, income and occupation." Unpublished Master's Thesis, Northwestern University, 1960.

Hunt, Morton. "Help wanted: divorce counseling." *The New York Times Magazine.* January 1:14-17, 1967.

Hunt, Morton. "Sexual behavior in the 1970's." *Playboy.* Volume 20, Number 10:83-88, 194-197,

October, 1973; Volume 20, Number 11:74-75, November 1973, Volume 20, Number 12:90-91, 256, December, 1973.

Hunt, Morton M. *The World of the Formerly Married.* New York: McGraw-Hall, 1966.

Institute of Life Insurance. Youth: Finance—Related Attitudes 1972, New York, 1973.

Ireland, Gordon and Galindez, Jesus de. *Divorce in the Americas.* Buffalo: Dennis, 1947.

Jacobson, Edmund, *Progressive Relaxation,* Chicago: University of Chicago Press, 1938.

Kay, Herma Hill. "A family court: the California proposal." In *Divorce and After,* ed. Paul Bohannan. New York: Doubleday Anchor, 1971. Pp. 243-282.

Kessler, Sheila. "Survey of emotional divorce." Georgia State Counseling Center, Monograph, 1974.

Kinsey, Alfred C.; Pomeroy, Wardell, B.; Martin, Clyde E.; and Gebhard, Paul. *Sexual Behavior in the Human Female.* Saunders, 1952. P. 442.

Kirpatrick, Clifford. "The changing status of women." *The Family: As Process and Institution.* New York: Ronald, 1963, 2nd edition.

Knox, David. *Marriage Happiness.* Chicago: Research Press, 1971.

Komarovsky, Mirra. *Blue Collar Marriage.* New York: Random House, 1964. Pp. 290-93.

Kranztler, Mel. *Creative Divorce.* New York: Evans, 1974.

Krishnan, P. "Divorce tables for females in the United States, 1960." *Journal of Marriage and the Family.* Volume 33, Number 2:318-320, May, 1971.

Krumboltz, John D. and Thoreson, Carl. *Behavioral Counseling: Case and Techniques.* New York. Holt, 1969.

Kübler-Ross, Elisabeth. *On Death and Dying.* New York: Macmillan, 1969.

Lasch, Christopher. "Divorce and the family in America." In *Search for Human Understanding: A Reader in Psychology,* ed. Michael Merbaum and George Stricker. New York: Holt, 1971.

Lasch, Christopher. "Easy divorce is a form of social insurance." In *Search for Human Understanding,* ed. Michael Merbaum and George Stricker. New York: Holt, 1971.

Lazarus, Arnold A. *Behavior Therapy and Beyond.* New York: McGraw-Hill, 1971.

Lederer, William J. and Jackson, Don D. *The Mirages of Marriage.* New York: Norton, 1968.

Leighton, D. C.; Harding, J. S.; Macklin, D. B.; Macmillan, A. M.; and Leighton, A. H. *The Character of Danger.* New York: Basic Books, 1963.

Lesse, Stanley. *Anxiety: Its Components, Development and Treatment.* New York: Grune and Stratton, 1970.

Levy, Robert. *Uniform Marriage and Divorce Legislation: A Preliminary Analysis:* Prepared for the special Committee of Commissioners of Uniform State Laws. Chicago, 1968.

Libby, Roger and Whitehurst, Robert. *Renovating Marriage.* California: Consensus Publishers, 1973.

Lichtenberger, J. P. *Divorce: A Social Interpretation.* New York: Arno, 1972.

Lieberman, Jethro K. *The Tyranny of the Experts.* Walker, New York, 1970.

Lief, Harold I. "Psychoneurotic disorders. I: anxiety, conversion, dissociative, and phobic reactions." In *Comprehensive Textbook of Psychiatry*, ed. Alfred M. Freedman and Harold I. Kaplan. Baltimore: Williams and Wilkins, 1967.

Lyness, Judith L.; Lipetz, Milton E.; and Davis, Keith. "Living together: An alternative to marriage." *Journal of Marriage and the Family*. May, 1972. Vol. 34, No. 2, pp. 305-311.

Lyon, Catherine Dillon and Saario, Terry N. "Women in public education: sexual discrimination in promotions." *Phi Delta Kappan*, Vol. LV, No. 2, October 1973, pp. 120-123.

Mariano, John. *The Use of Psychotherapy in Divorce and Separation Cases.* New York: American Press, 1958.

Maslow, A. H. *Motivation and Personality.* New York: Harper, 1954.

May, Rollo. *Love and Will.* New York: Dell, 1973.

Mercer, Charles. "Interrelations among family stability, family composition, residence and race." *Journal of Marriage and the Family.* Volume 29, No. 3, August, 1967. Pp. 456-460.

Mendels, Joseph. *Concepts of Depression.* New York: Wiley, 1970.

Mead, Margaret. "Anomalies in American postdivorce relationships." In *Divorce and After,* ed. Paul Bohannan. New York: Doubleday Anchor, 1971.

Miller, Arthur. "Reactions of friends to divorce." In *Divorce and After,* ed. Paul Bohannan. New York: Doubleday Anchor, 1971.

Miller, Neal E. and Dollard, John. *Social Learning and Imitation.* New Haven: Yale University Press, 1941.

Monahan, Thomas P. and Kephart, William M. "Divorce and desertion by religious and mixed-religious groups." *American Journal of Sociology.* Volume 59: 454-465, 1954.

Mortlock, Bill. *The Inside of Divorce: A Critical Examination of the System.* London: Constable, 1972.

Moustakas, Clark E. *Loneliness.* Englewood Cliffs, N.J.: Prentice-Hall, 1961.

Oho, Herbert. "Communes: The alternative life style." *Saturday Review,* Volume 54, April 24, 1971. Pp. 16-21.

O'Neill, Nena and O'Neill, George. *Open Marriage: A New Life Style for Couples.* New York: Evans, 1972.

O'Neill, William. *Divorce in the Progressive Era.* New Haven: Yale University Press, 1967.

Opler, Marvin K. "Woman's social status and the forms of marriage." *American Journal of Sociology.* Volume XLIX, Number 2:125-146, September, 1943.

Paget, Norman W. and Kein, Marcella. *Counseling Services to Parents and Children Involved in Divorce Proceedings: A Report on the Use of Assertive Casework Techniques.* San Bernadino, Calif.: July, 1960.

Parker, Rolland S. *Emotional Common Sense: How to Avoid Self-Destructiveness.* New York: Harper, 1973.

Pollitt, John. *Depression and Its Treatment.* Springfield, Illinois: Thomas, 1965.

Popham, James W. *Educational Statistics: Use and Interpretation.* New York: Harper, 1967.

Porteous, Hedy S. *Sex and Identity: Your Child's Sexuality.* New York: Bobbs-Merril, 1972.

Rainwater, Lee; Coleman, Richard; and Handel, Gerald. *Workingman's Wife: Her Personality, World and Life Style.* New York: Oceana, 1959.

Ramey, James W. "Communes, group marriage, and the upper middle class." *Journal of Marriage and the Family.* Vol. 34, Number 4:647-655, November, 1972.

Renne, Karen S. "Health and marital experience in an urban population." *Journal of Marriage and the Family.* Volume 33, Number 2:338-350, May, 1971.

Rheinstein, Max. *Marriage Stability, Divorce, and the Law.* Chicago: University of Chicago Press, 1972.

Rheinstein, Max. "Divorce law in Sweden." In *Divorce and After,* ed. Paul Bohannan. New York: Doubleday Anchor, 1971. Pp. 143-170.

Roach, Jack L. and Gursslin, Orville R. "The lower class, status frustration, and social disorganization." *Social Forces.* Volume 43, Number 1: October, 1965.

Rodman, Hyman. "The lower-class value stretch." *Social Forces.* Volume 42: 205-215, 1963.

Rogers, Carl. *Becoming Partners.* New York: Delacorte, 1972.

Rokeach, Milton. *The Nature of Human Values.* New York: Free Press, 1973.

Roleder, George. *Marriage Means Encounter.* Dubuque, Iowa: William C. Brown, 1973.

Rosow, Irving and Rose, K. Daniel. "Divorce among doctors." *Journal of Marriage and the Family.* Volume 32, Number 4:587-599, November, 1972.

Rycroft, Charles. *Anxiety and Neurosis.* London: Penguin Books, 1970.

Scanzoni, John. "A reinquiry into marital disorganization." *Journal of Marriage and the Family.* Volume 30, Number 3:452-461, August 1968.

Scanzoni, John. "A social system analysis of dissolved and existing marriages." *Journal of Marriage and the Family.* Volume 30, Number 3: 452-461, August 1968.

Schacter, Stanley and Singer, Jerome. "Cognitive, social and physiological determinants of emotional state." In *Behavior Change Through Self-Control,* ed. Marvin R. Goldried and Michael Merbaum. New York: Holt, 1973.

Scott, John Paul and Fuller, John L. *Genetics and the Social Behavior of the Dog.* Chicago: University of Chicago Press, 1965.

Sheresky, Norman and Mannes, Marya. *Uncoupling: The Art of Coming Apart.* New York: Viking, 1972.

Smith, T. Lynn. *Brazil: People and Institutions.* Baton Rouge: Louisiana State University Press, 1963. Pp. 459-483.

Steiner, Lee. *Romantic Marriage: 20th Century Illusion.* Radner, Pa.: Chilton, 1963.

Stekel, Wilhelm. *Compulsion and Doubt.* New York: Washington Square Press, 1949.

Talmon, Yonuna. *Family and Community in the Kibbutz.* Cambridge, Mass.: Harvard University Press, 1972.

Toffler, Alvin. *Future Shock.* New York: Random House, 1970.

U.S. Bureau of the Census. "Marriage and Divorce: 1887-1906." Department of Commerce and Labor. Bulletin 96, Government Printing Office, Washington, D.C.

U.S. Bureau of the Census. "U.S. Census Population: 1960, Subject Reports, Marital Status, Final Report." PC(2)—4E; table 5. Government Printing Office, Washington, D.C.

U.S. Bureau of the Census. "Statistical Abstract of the United States: 1972." 93rd Edition. Government Printing Office, Washington, D.C.

U.S. Bureau of the Census. "Population Trends in the United States: 1900 to 1960." Technical Paper Number 10. U.S. Government Printing Office, Washington, D.C., 1964.

U.S. News and World Report. "Women: more jobs, but low pay." Volume LXXV, Number 15:41-42. October 8, 1973.

U.S. News and World Report. "Group living catches on and goes middle class." Volume LXXVI, Number 8:38-43, February 25, 1974.

U.S. Public Health Service. "Annual Summary for the United States: 1971: Births, Deaths, Marriages and Divorces." *Monthly Vital Statistics Report.* Vol. 20, Number 13. (HSM) 72-1121, August 30, 1972. Government Printing Office, Washington, D.C.

U.S. Public Health Service. "Annual Summary for the United States, 1972." *Monthly Vital Statistics Report.* Vol. 21, Number 13. (HSM) 73-1121, June 27, 1973. Government Printing Office, Washington, D.C.

U.S. Public Health Service. "Divorces: Analysis of Change: United States 1969." From U.S. Department of Health, Education and Welfare. Number 22, Series 21. (HSM) 73-1900. Government Printing Office, Washington, D.C.

U.S. Public Health Service. "Increases in Divorces: United States—1967." *Vital and Health Statistics.* Series 21, Number 20, Publication Number 1000. December 1970. Government Printing Office, Washington, D.C.

U.S. Public Health Service. "Marriages: Trends and Characteristics: United States." *Vital and Health Statistics.* Series 21, Number 21, DHEW Publication Number (HSM) 72-1007, Septermber, 1971. Government Printing Office, Washington, D.C.

U.S. Public Health Service. "Mortality from Selected Causes by Marital Status: United States—Part A." *Vital and Health Statistics.* Series 20, Number 8, Pp. 36-51. Government Printing Office, Washington, D.C.

U.S. Public Health Service. "Selected Symptoms of Psychological Distress." *Vital and Health Statistics.* Number 1000, Series 11, Number 37, August 1970. Government Printing Office, Washington, D.C.

U.S. Public Health Service. "Vital Statistics Rates in the United States 1940-1960." *Vital and Health Statistics.* Publication Number 1677. Government Printing Office, Washington, D.C.

U.S. Public Health Service. "Vital Statistics of the United States, 1969, Volume III: Marriage and Divorce." *Vital and Health Statistics.* Number (HSM) 73-1103, 1972. Government Printing Office, Washington, D.C.

U.S. Public Health Service. "Divorce Statistics, 1966." January 6, 1969, Government Printing Office, Washington, D.C.

U.S. Public Health Service "Divorce Statistics, 1969."

Monthly Vital Statistics Report, Volume 20, Number 4, Supplement (2), July 22, 1971. Government Printing Office, Washington, D.C.

U.S. Public Health Service. "Divorce Statistics Analysis: United States, 1964 and 1965." Series 21, Number 17. Government Printing Office, Washington, D.C.

U.S. Women's Bureau. "Women Workers Today." From U.S. Department of Labor Employment Standards Administration. 1973. Government Printing Office, Washington, D.C.

Veroff, Joseph, and Feld, Sheila. *Marriage and Work in America: A Study of Motives and Roles.* New York: Van Nostrand Reinhold, 1970.

Waters, Harry. "Games singles play." *Newsweek.* July 16, 1973:52-58.

Weisman, Avery D. *On Dying and Denying.* New York: Behavioral Publications, 1972.

Wheelis, Allen. *The Quest for Identity.* New York: Norton, 1958.

White, Mervin and Wells, Carolyn "Student attitudes toward alternative marriage forms." In *Renovating Marriage,* ed. Roger W. Libby and Robert Whitehurst. California: Consensus Publishers, 1973.

Whitehurst, Robert N. "Youth views marriage: Some comparisons of two generation attitudes of university students." In *Renovating Marriage,* ed. Roger W. Libby and Robert Whitehurst. California: Consensus Publishers, 1973.

Winch, Robert F. *The Modern Family,* rev. ed. New York: Holt, 1963.

Wolpe, Joseph, M.D. *The Practice of Behavior Therapy.* New York: Pergammon, 1969.

Wolpe, Joseph; Salter, Andrew; and Reyna, L. J. *The Conditioning Therapies: The Challenge in Psychotherapy.* New York: Holt, 1964.

The World Almanac and Book of Facts: 1974. Edited by George Delury. New York: Newspaper Enterprise Association, 1973.

Yates, Aubrey J. *Frustration and Conflict.* New York: Wiley, 1962.

Index

Women (continued)
and freedom, 164-65
in government, 167
as heads of household, 188
income of, 166
and remarriage, 167
self-identity of, 168
single, with child, 188-89
special problems of, 155
status of, 115
in work force, 166-70
working-class, 168-69

Yoga, 50

Zwingli, Huldreich, 152